Clyde Coastal Path Gui...

Clyde Coastal Path

To Sally,

with many thanks.

Vincent Cuddihy

Clyde Coastal Path Guidebook

Ceum-coise

Linne

Chuaidh

Forward!   Photograph: Stuart Sharkie

Clyde Coastal Path

A Guidebook

by

Vincent Cuddihy

Clyde Coastal Path Rotary

Clyde Coastal Path Guidebook

This Guidebook describes for walkers, with or without dogs, the Clyde Coastal Path which runs from the Kelly Burn (the border with Ayrshire) to Milngavie. For information about further connecting paths, see Appendix I.

The Partick Spur, the Paisley Spur and use by cyclists and horses will be covered in future. For details about the future development of the Clyde Coastal Path, see Appendix II.

Clyde Coastal Path Guidebook is Printed and Published in Scotland by the Clyde Coastal Path Board of the Rotary Clubs of Allander, Erskine, Govan, Gourock, Paisley Callants and Renfrew.

© Clyde Coastal Path Board

All rights reserved.

No part of this publication may be reproduced, stored in a retrieval system, or transmitted, in any form or by any means without the prior written permission of the publisher, nor be otherwise circulated in any form of binding or cover other than that in which it is published and without a similar condition being imposed on the subsequent purchaser.

First Printed 2018 June

ISBN: 978-1-84500-300-5

Information about the Clyde Coastal Path can be found at

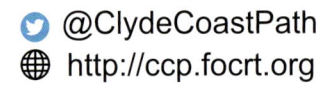

@ClydeCoastPath
http://ccp.focrt.org

Please send comments to ccp@focrt.org

Clyde Coastal Path
Rotary

Clyde Coastal Path Guidebook

For my wife, Avril, who walked every metre of the Clyde Coastal Path with me in the pursuit of the interesting snippets which populate these pages.

Vincent

Clyde Coastal Path Guidebook

Acknowledgments

I would like to give a special thanks to Iain White, a fellow Allander Rotarian, without whom there would be no book. He has designed and produced the book, as well as meticulously proof reading.

I am indebted to Jim Adamson and Jim Blair of Gourock Rotary. They are walking encyclopaedias on all things Gourockian and Greenockian, and just about everywhere else between Wemyss Bay and the Erskine Bridge. Jim Blair sacrificed many days walking and driving me along the Path.

Thank you to Professor Emeritus James Dickson FRSE for a most enjoyable and informative afternoon exploring the lime dumps alongside the Allander water.

A special thanks to David Palmar, whose keen eye, knowledge of geography, wildlife, grammar and so much more besides, was invaluable.

Many thanks to David Carnduff for his invaluable help with the birdlife in the Kelly Glen and the Kelly and Greenock Cuts. Jean and Iain Macdonald gave up a morning to walk me through the Craigton section of the walk and supplied coffee and biscuits.

Thanks to Iain MacVoy for articles and booklets that helped my research.

Thanks to Gil Paterson, MSP, and Jo Sherington, West Dunbartonshire Council, for help with the image of the Cochno Stone. Thanks, also, to Iain MacDonald for the interesting discussions about Scots Gaelic.

To the following: Malcolm Boddie – Milngavie and Bearsden camera club for many helpful suggestions in running and judging the Photographic Competition; all the participants in the Competition, even if work not used; Glengoyne Distillery for sponsoring the Photographic Competition. Thanks to David Atkinson of CO2 Design for useful contributions to layout and design.

Finally heartfelt thanks to Rotary District 1230 for their grant to help publish the book.

Clyde Coastal Path Guidebook

Contents

Acknowledgments	6
Foreword	**9**
Introduction to the Clyde Coastal Path	11
About Rotary	12
Some Sample Signs	13
Explanation of Coloured Text	13
1. Wemyss Bay to Lunderston Bay - Coastal Route	15
2. Lunderston Bay to Greenock Esplanade	23
3. Greenock Esplanade to Victoria Harbour	33
4. Wemyss Bay to Victoria Harbour - Muirland Route	43
5. Victoria Harbour to Woodhall Roundabout	55
6. Woodhall Roundabout to Erskine Bridge	71
7. Erskine Bridge to Hardgate	83
8. Hardgate to the Stockiemuir Road	95
9. Craigton to Milngavie	107
Appendix I. Further Connections	**119**
A. Firth o Clyde Rotary Trail (Opened 9 May 2015)	119
B. West Highland Way	120
C. Cape Wrath Trail	121
D. John Galt Way	121
Appendix II. Further Developments	**123**
A. Path Development	123
B. IT Development	123
The Rotary Family	124
Appendix III. Rotary Family and CCP Board	**124**
Clyde Coastal Path Board	124
The Rotary Family	124
Index	**125**
List of Images	137
List of Maps	138
About the Author	139

Clyde Coastal Path Guidebook

Introduction

Foreword

In May 2015, I had the honour of standing up in the middle of Milngavie precinct and opening the Firth o Clyde Rotary Trail. It brings together three long-distance walks: the Mull of Galloway Trail, the Ayrshire Coastal Path and the Clyde Coastal Path. Living only a few miles from Milngavie, I've needed exactly what this guidebook provides to get me started on the last of these, which ends, or begins, on my very doorstep.

The Clyde Coastal Path takes us on a 36-mile journey from Wemyss Bay to the village of Milngavie via the Erskine Bridge. As well as keeping us on the right track, the guidebook wonderfully evokes the influence that the River Clyde has had, and still has, on the communities it passes through. It highlights the gorgeous, diverse scenery en route and documents some fascinating social and natural history. I love all the stories.

Following the Clyde Coastal Path combines the joys of the outdoors with a celebration of everything we love most about Scotland. Hand me those walking boots!

Sally Magnusson
Broadcaster and author

Clyde Coastal Path Guidebook

Introduction

Introduction to the Clyde Coastal Path

"Oh the River Clyde the wonderful Clyde
The name of it thrills me and fills me with pride
And I'm satisfied whate'er may betide
The sweetest of songs is the song of the Clyde"

At the start of the Clyde Coastal Path, in Wemyss Bay, you are at the Firth of Clyde, the mouth of the River Clyde at the end of its 109 mile long journey (176 km) from its distant rising in the Lowther Hills in South Lanarkshire. It is formed by the Daer Water and the Potrail Water at the Watermeetings and is the second longest river in Scotland, after the Tay, and is the eighth largest in the United Kingdom. In Scots Gaelic it is called, Abhainn Chluaidh, in Scots, Watter o Clyde and was known as Clud or Clut in the early medieval Cumbric language.

The Clyde Coastal Path, as well as taking you on a 34 to 36 mile journey, depending on the route chosen (coast or muirland), it is taking you on journey through places that although different in character, are linked. It is a journey of connections. There is the physical connection of the south side of the path to the north side via the Erskine Bridge. Both sides of the bridge are connected by famous people; by the effects of the Industrial Revolution and subsequent post industrial decline; by wars, including the American Civil War, World War One and World War Two and by the legacies of Prehistoric and Roman times.

Common throughout the journey is the evidence of the power of water and the water itself. Rivers that rise in different points on the path all eventually empty into the Clyde. The water you see here at

Clyde Coastal Path Guidebook

the Firth of Clyde once also ran in the Duntocher Burn and the Allander Water and its tributaries.

The path offers diverse scenery, sometimes stunning, always beautiful.

The Clyde Coastal Path was devised and marked out by the Rotary Club of Gourock and the Rotary Club of Allander (Bearsden and Milngavie) and was officially opened in 2014. It is a joint Rotary community project to promote fitness and health while encouraging the exploration of scenic Scotland.

This guide book directs the way ahead but also tells some of the social, natural and developmental history of Scotland and her people. Although this Guidebook describes the route from Wemyss Bay to Milngavie, the Clyde Coastal Path is bidirectional. Further information about the Rotary Clubs involved in the Path and the Rotary family can be found in Appendix III.

About Rotary

Paul Harris was brought up in small town America before moving to Chicago to practise law. As he experienced the isolation of the stranger in a large city, he arranged with three other friends to meet at regular intervals in each other's premises on a rotational basis- hence the concept of "Rotary". They held their first meeting on 23 February 1905 and within the first year were actively involved in service to the community. From that small beginning Rotary International has grown to be the world's largest service organisation with 1.2 million members in over 200 countries.

Rotary's motto – Service Above Self – succinctly summarises the aim of Rotary, namely, to raise funds and donate time and skills to help those in need at local, national and international level.

"Walking is man's best medicine."
Hippocrates

Introduction

Some Sample Signs

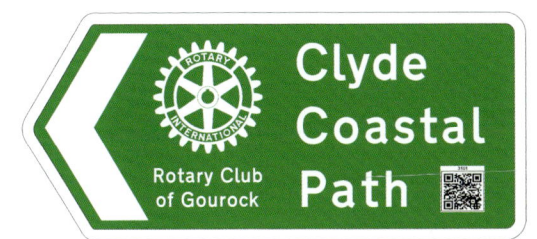

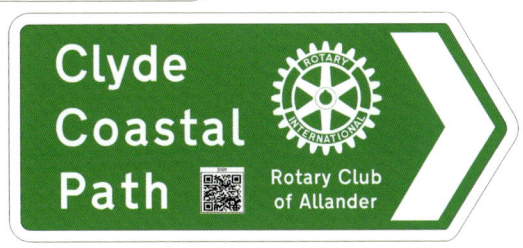

Throughout your journey you will see many signs, particularly the above. They are designed to keep you on the straight and narrow and reassure you when the path is neither.

In future, you might also see the thistle sign, left. This symbol acknowledges that you are on a path designated as one of Scotland's Great Trails.

Explanation of Coloured Text

The following Colour Scheme is used throughout this book:

Directions are in Blue
Points of interest/information Black
Nature notes are Green
Alternative route Orange
Danger Red
Quotations Burgundy

Clyde Coastal Path Guidebook

1. Wemyss Bay to Lunderston Bay - Coastal Route

14

Chapter 1. Wemyss Bay to Lunderston Bay

1. Wemyss Bay to Lunderston Bay - Coastal Route

"A durum a doo a dum a day
A durum ado ma daddy O
A durum a doo a dum a day
The day we went to Rothesay O"

The Clyde Coastal Path starts in the middle of the bridge over the Kelly Burn. The Low Coastal Route passes through the village of Wemyss Bay.

Wemyss Bay Station   Photograph: Iain R White

Wemyss Bay is adjacent to Skelmorlie. These two villages are in different counties; the former in Renfrewshire and the latter in North Ayrshire, separated by the Kelly Burn.

Wemyss Bay was created as a "marine village" and watering place in the 19th century by Robert Wallace of Kelly. Wallace was elected Greenock's first MP in 1832 and served until 1836. He was a Whig franchise reformer and agitated for postal service reform. His casting

Clyde Coastal Path Guidebook

vote as chairman of the committee examining, Rowland Hill's Penny Postage scheme, resulted in the scheme's being recommended to Parliament.

The name Wemyss derives from the Scots Gaelic word uaimh that translates as cave and is believed to have been taken from the caves and cliffs of the Firth of Forth in that part of Fife where the clan Wemyss made its home. Wemyss in Fife has been the seat of the chiefs since the 12th century. However, I am attracted to the alternative legend that it was simply named after Bob Wemyss who was an owner of a hut on the shore in the 19th century.

The village was developed further by a London merchant, James Alexander, when he built a steamboat pier. Both this pier and its successor were swept away by hurricanes and replaced by a railway terminal and pier. In 1865, the Port Glasgow to Wemyss Bay Railway opened to connect to the Clyde steamer services for Rothesay, Largs and Millport, and the Isle of Cumbrae. The Wemyss Bay Steamboat Company was formed to own the connecting steamers. It operated a paddle steamer to take businessmen from Lamlash on the Isle of Arran and also from Tighnabruaich to connect with trains to Glasgow. Today the station incorporates the Caledonian MacBrayne ferry terminal connecting the mainland to Rothesay on the Isle of Bute.

It is well worth spending a little time in the Wemyss Bay station and enjoy this A-listed Edwardian styled building, designed in 1903 by James Miller. Elegant glass canopies with graceful steel curves provide protection from the rain during the walk from the train to the ferry for Rothesay. A substantial refurbishment project

New Arrivals
Photograph: Matt Johnston

Chapter 1. Wemyss Bay to Lunderston Bay

was carried out by Graham and Sibbald on behalf of Caledonian Maritime Assets Limited (CMAL), and won the 2017 RICS (Royal Institution of Chartered Surveyors) Scotland Award for Infrastructure.

Also before you set off, take a look at the stunning views of the Clyde. On a clear day you can see Arran and clearly pick out Gaoda Bheinn, more commonly known as Goatfell. At 2867 ft / 874 m, it is the tallest of the four Corbetts on Arran. The Sleeping Warrior can also be seen. The name is a description, from the mainland, of the profile of the hills of north Arran. The profile begins with the Witch's Step as the face, Caisteal Abhail (2818 ft / 859 m), the second highest Corbett, as the folded arms, and continues along the ridge towards Meall Mòr in the direction of Lochranza and Catacol.

When you come out of the station turn left and north, unless you feel the need for refreshment. In which case cross the road to the Seaview Café.

This is a well established café that was taken over by Nigel Owen, owner of the adjoining shop, Mearns T McCaskie, and reopened as a sit in or take away café and a bistro. If you are planning to camp and eat al fresco and feeling adventurous, perhaps you should drop into Mearns T McCaskie, butcher for over 80 years and 2015 Haggis Champion.

Walk along the pavement. After about a mile pass the very attractive red sandstone St Joseph's and St Patrick's church. At this point trees obscure the view of the Clyde. Carry straight on at junction with Ardgowan Road. Turn left down Mill Farm Road and at the bottom veer right up the hill that leads up to the main road. At the give way sign, continue on the path as it veers left and carries on behind a crash barrier alongside the main road. The Clyde is now in full view as Inverkip approaches.

Clyde Coastal Path Guidebook

Inverkip has an interesting history although now is a mainly residential village, including a very large number of houses on the hill above.

It was created a "burgh of barony" before the Acts of Union in 1707, meaning that the Laird or landowner could hold a weekly market. At that time the parish included Skelmorlie, Wemyss Bay, all of Gourock and a part of Greenock. The 17th century laird, Alexander Lindsay of Dunrod, was infamous both for the killing of a brother-in-law of Patrick Maxwell, owner of Newark Castle, and also because he was believed to be in league with the devil. He was referred to as Auld Dunrod and was the last of the Lindsay family of Dunrod Castle. Due to his dissolute ways he lost all his possessions and became involved in the black arts.

"In Auld Kirk the witches ride thick

And in Dunrod they dwell;

But the greatest among them a'

Is Auld Dunrod himsel'."

He died in mysterious circumstances in a barn belonging to one of his previous tenant farmers. Nothing remains of Dunrod Castle. It was located near Shielhill Farm in the Clyde Muirshiel Regional Park.

Inverkip also once had an oil fired power station which dominated the area with its 778 ft (237 m) chimney; third tallest chimney in UK and Scotland's tallest free standing structure. It had no cooling tower and used seawater as coolant. This much missed landmark, used as a navigation mark, was demolished on 28 July 2013 as part of the demolition of the power station started in 2010 to make way for housing and small businesses.

Chapter 1. Wemyss Bay to Lunderston Bay

Kip Marina   Photograph: Peter Smith

Continue on and turn left into Kip Marina. The Marina contains both a café and a restaurant. Turn first left and then left again for the Café Riva. The Chartroom Restaurant is straight ahead on left.

Kip Marina is the first purpose built marina in Scotland and plays host to Scotland's Boat Show every October. Construction started in the late 1960s and the first phase was completed in 1971. It was originally planned for 250 berths but by 1984 had expanded to provide 600 berths and additionally accommodates 150 boats as hard standing on cradles.

If not stopping for refreshment, cross the road and continue over the bridge then veer right. The path straight ahead is a private road into the Ardgowan Estate. Go left and then as indicated by repeater sign turn left. Continue and turn left again. The next bit of path tends to collect large puddles. Continue through a wooded area, then down

Clyde Coastal Path Guidebook

left and turn right at a T-junction. This path continues along the coast all the way to Lunderston Bay.

Lunderston Bay   Photograph: Iain R White

Peewit
Photograph: David Palmar
photoscot.co.uk

LOOK OUT and LISTEN FOR a wide variety of woodland and shore birds. The species on view vary with the season. In winter, grebes and divers gather. Gannets perform their high-speed spectacular plummet into the water, and if it is calm, porpoises and basking sharks may be seen. Guillemots and razorbills have been observed. Along the shores, the noisy oystercatchers join curlews and redshanks while further out are rafts of eiders. Curlews, with their long distinctive down curving bill and burbling trilling "cor-lee" call, have unfortunately been in decline generally of late. Lapwings, often

Chapter 1. Wemyss Bay to Lunderston Bay

known as peewits in imitation of their call, may be seen. These once familiar farmland and shore birds are also in decline and are now a Red List species. In the woodlands, there is a variety of tits, robins and thrushes. Listen out for the "teacher, teacher" call of the great tit or is it just the opening and closing of a squeaky gate? The distinctive mewing sound of buzzards and the repeated deep guttural croaking "krrro, krrro krrro" of ravens may also be heard.

As you walk along, enjoy the spectacular views across the Firth of Clyde. On clear days, you can look across to Dunoon, Innellan and the hills of the Cowal Peninsula. Look down the Clyde to the Isles of Bute and Arran. Further up are the hills of Argyll. The sandy beach is very popular for days out and picnics. Lunderston Bay holds very fond memories for many Scots.

Halfway across the car park at Lunderston Bay there is a concrete bin beside stairs leading up to the main road. This is the safest crossing to the Cardwell Garden Centre as this spot allows good views in both directions of the traffic.

Buzzard Hovering

Photograph: David Palmar
photoscot.co.uk

The Garden Centre caters for the home and garden and was established by Eric Gallagher in 1962 and continues to be family operated. It has expanded and now offers 9 acres of retail space and 10 acres of nursery facilities. There are 20 departments – just how big is your haversack? The restaurant serves a wide variety of food.

Clyde Coastal Path Guidebook

2. Lunderston Bay to Greenock Esplanade

Chapter 2. Lunderston Bay to Greenock Espanade

2. Lunderston Bay to Greenock Esplanade

Continue through the car park to the green building at the end that houses public toilets that are however not always open. Pass to the left of green building, follow the path round and turn left on to the main road: A770 / Cloch Road. Continue until you come to the Cloch Lighthouse sitting right on the edge of the pavement.

This road is known as the Cloch Road and is named after a lighthouse. Despite knowing this it is still an arresting sight to see a lighthouse rising 76 ft from the edge of the pavement at Cloch Point. The name Cloch (modern form clach) is a Scots Gaelic word; stone in English.

The lighthouse, designed by Robert Smith and his son-in-law Robert Stevenson, was completed in 1797. Stevenson, who also built many bridges, was part of a lighthouse building dynasty which included his brothers, sons and nephews. Together, they were responsible for the erection of more than eighty lighthouses.

He was also the grandfather of Robert Louis Stevenson who declined to pursue a career in engineering and became a prolific writer of short stories, novels, essays, poetry, non-fiction and music. The future author was described as an unusual child, both in appearance and behaviour and went on to live a bohemian life style, much to the disappointment and horror of his mother and father.

Smith and Stevenson installed the first ever oil lantern in the Cloch. The acetylene light was replaced by an Argand and silvered reflector in 1829 and then in 1931, a radio beacon was installed. A foghorn was installed between 1895 and 1897. In the 1990s, the main light was closed down and replaced by an optic mounted on a pole just outside the lantern. Ships now use a buoyed channel. The keepers' houses are now private residencies.

Clyde Coastal Path Guidebook

The first small, square, white building before (west of) the lighthouse was the magazine for a 6 inch gun emplaced on a concrete base on the east side of the lighthouse. The gun guarded the Firth of Clyde and the river boom during World War Two. The base for the gun is easily seen. It has been slightly modified to provide a vantage point.

The Cloch Lighthouse had a range of 14 miles (23 km) and was paired with the Gantocks Light at Dunoon to warn ships entering the Clyde about the Gantocks Reef. This skerry, a Norse word for rock, is just visible above the water but at night and in stormy or foggy weather ships foundered.

The Cloch Light   Photograph: John MacLeod

Chapter 2. Lunderston Bay to Greenock Espanade

In the 19th century, the distance between the Cloch and Little Cumbrae lighthouse was used for time trials. The practice of 'Running the Lights' became an event on the Clyde for any new steamer. A fast ship could run the distance, approximately 16 miles, in 48 minutes.

Despite lights, whistles, foghorn and buoys, accidents still happen. In 1956, MV Akka, a Swedish long ore carrier struck the rocks when her steering gear failed. Three crew went down with her and three died later in hospital. Twenty seven members of the crew were rescued. In 1977, the paddle steamer PS Waverley was grounded but fortunately got free and was able to be repaired and still can be seen on the Clyde today.

Dunoon is directly across and there are lovely views of Loch Long making Cloch Point an excellent site for viewing the Clyde. Further on, on the opposite side of the road, are new flats offering wonderful views over the Clyde. Behind the flats are several factories and a very large distribution centre belonging to Amazon. The area is called Faulds Park.

There are opportunities to catch sight of Manx shearwaters and auks . Sandwich terns have been reported, as have cormorants and shags. Other seabirds including guillemots and razorbills, have also been spotted.

A little further on is McInroy's Point.

This is a small peninsula in the west of Gourock. In the early 1970s, a pier was constructed to form the departure point for Western Ferries to Hunter's Quay, near Dunoon, offering a second service crossing the Clyde, directly to Dunoon. It operates in competition with Caledonian MacBrayne's foot passenger only service to Dunoon, leaving from further up the coast. Western Ferries is a faster

Clyde Coastal Path Guidebook

PS Waverley   Photograph: Matt Johnston

crossing and can accommodate vehicular traffic, providing motorists with a rapid gateway to the Scottish Highlands.

In April 2018, passengers travelling between Gourock and Dunoon have been enthralled by what has been labelled, "Urban Orcas".

A pod of killer whales were seen leaping out of the water. Experts reported that they are regularly seen off the Isle of Arran on the Firth of Clyde but have not been regular visitors to the Upper Clyde for many years. The waters are rich in delicious porpoises and seals. Many observers on the beach enjoyed the spectacle through their binoculars. Dolphins have been spotted along the Clyde but are much less common.

Continue along Cloch Road past the Royal Gourock Yacht Club, founded in 1894 when it was entitled the Gourock Sailing Club.

Chapter 2. Lunderston Bay to Greenock Espanade

It changed its name in 1900 to the Gourock Yacht Club. James Coats, one of the famous thread-making family, donated funds to build a new clubhouse in its present position in 1902, offering superb views over the Clyde and the Argyll hills. Many of his family were keen sailors. King Edward VII in 1908 assented for it to be renamed 'royal'. It is now the weekly meeting place of the Rotary Club of Gourock.

After a couple of hundred yards further on, turn down on to the walkway running alongside the main road. On the left, pass Gourock swimming pool and fitness gym.

The pool is one of the last open air pools in Scotland. It was built in 1909 and had a sandy floor and was tidal. Exposed to the elements it was cold and being tidal it also was the bearer of flotsam and jetsam, some of an unpleasant nature. However it has been completely refurbished, the pool has been raised and now has clean heated seawater. Aren't you glad you packed your swimming costume?

After the pool, proceed down left to Lower Kempock Street and walk alongside the car park. Enjoy the splendid views as you make your way towards Gourock Railway Station and the Kilcreggan Ferry.

"Lookin' oot across the watter
when 'tis dark as dark can be,
When there's not a whiff o wind
to break the stillness o the sea,
When the air is clear and frosty
'tis the cheerfulest o sights
To behold the scores an' hundreds
o the twinkling Gourock lights!"

Clyde Coastal Path Guidebook

The name Gourock comes from the Scots Gaelic word Guireag, a pimple. More kindly people may extend the translation to mean rounded hill, many of which surround the town. History records that King James IV sailed from the shore at Gourock to quell the rebellious Highland Clans. Initially a small fishing village, it expanded and became involved in herring curing, copper mining, quarrying and ropemaking. Latterly it became involved in yacht making and repairing. The Gourock Rope Works was founded in 1711 and bought over the Port Glasgow Rope and Duct Company and moved to Port Glasgow.

In 1889, the Caledonian Railway made its way to Gourock to service the pier and the Caledonian Steam Packet Company, now part of Caledonian MacBrayne. In the latter half of the nineteenth century and first half of the twentieth century Gourock had its tourist heyday.Crowds set sail from the Broomielaw Quay in Glasgow or took the train along the coast to holiday, traditionally during the Glasgow Fair or spend the day in Gourock.

"And so we're goin' doon the watter
Ach we're goin' doon the watter fur the ferr"

The town lies between the river and high hills. It is mainly built on the beach front and only sparsely on the hills, hence the saying, "A tae ane side like Gourock".

The TS Queen Mary II, the Duchess of Hamilton and the Glen Sannox were much loved steamers offering sails "doon the watter".

Ahead the crown steeple of the St John's Church dominates Gourock. A small diversion towards this leads to "Granny Kempock's Stone". This is a six foot tall Megalithic stone behind Kempock Street which resembles an old woman. At one time this was a prominent object on the hillside, well known to ships passing on the river. It is now surrounded by buildings between Kempock Street and Castle

Chapter 2. Lunderston Bay to Greenock Espanade

Granny Kempock's Stone   Photograph: Paul Maiolani

Gardens. There was a superstition that for sailors going on long voyages or couples about to be married, walking round the stone seven times would ensure good fortune.

There is a route through the station but sometimes this is locked. If so, turn right alongside the station then left and left again into the station. Carry straight on as far as you can go and turn right. At the sign for ferries and Kilcreggan turn right. Again the pathway may be locked, in which case walk along the station platform until you meet the path.

Before making for the platform it is well worth a look at the exhibition on the left hand wall. This shows pictures of famous ferries of the past and a history board tells of the maritime wartime history of the station and pier.

The pathway leads to the Kilcreggan Ferry that is operated by Caledonian MacBrayne. This carries passengers only, to Dunoon. Walk alongside the Calmac offices and continue past them, staying on the right until you reach a large signpost welcoming travellers to the ferry. Cross over on to pavement. Continue and turn left and walk round Battery Park.

The name, Battery Park, comes from the coastal gun emplacement or battery that was built at Fort Matilda to defend Greenock against a possible attack by Napoleon's navy. The excavated material from the construction of a tunnel at Fort Matilda railway station was used as land fill to the west of the old gun emplacement of Fort Matilda forming a level area that became the playing field of Battery Park.

Follow the path alongside the water. Pass the brightly coloured children's play park, past the Battery Park Pavilion and Nursery. After the last building turn right alongside the red brick building, the old torpedo factory.

In 1907, the Admiralty compulsorily purchased part of this land and constructed the Clyde Torpedo Factory that opened in 1910. Seven hundred workers were transferred from the Royal Arsenal, Woolwich. The site was tasked with designing and testing torpedoes. Following World War Two, in 1947, the site became fully committed to research and development as the Torpedo Experimental Establishment (TEE). This was closed in 1959 when all torpedo research and development and design were concentrated at the newly formed Admiralty Underwater Weapons Establishment, Portland.

The long, low red brick building still stands and is occupied by a number of small businesses.

Chapter 2. Lunderston Bay to Greenock Espanade

Continue alongside the brick building and then turn left on to the main road. After about 500 yards turn left on to the Esplanade. There are new flats on the Esplanade on the site of the old Naval Buildings. You then pass the West of Scotland Amateur Sailing Club. The Esplanade is about 1 mile long and offers fine views of the Clyde and the hills.

Manx Shearwater

Photograph:
David Palmar
photoscot.co.uk

Rotary strives to make a difference locally, nationally and internationally.

Clyde Coastal Path
Rotary

Clyde Coastal Path Guidebook

3. Greenock Esplanade to Victoria Harbour

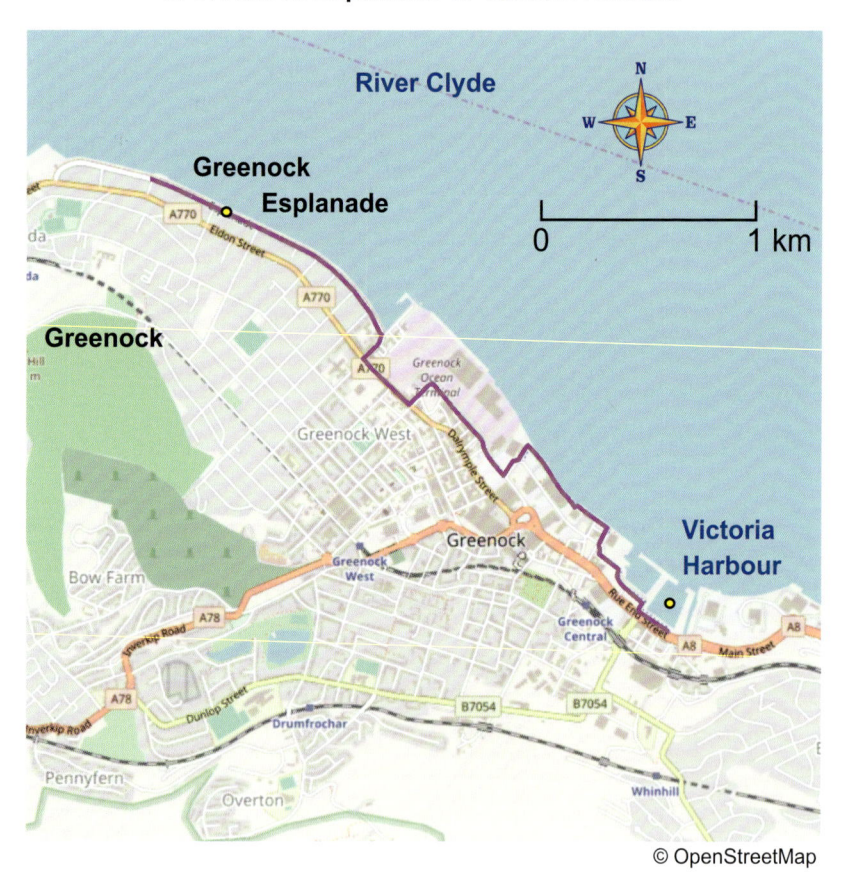

Chapter 3. Greenock Esplanade to Victoria Harbour

3. Greenock Esplanade to Victoria Harbour

Stroll along and enjoy the wonderful views of the Clyde that the houses on the other side of the road look on to. Initially, their gardens ran down to the shore before the material dug out of the Albert Harbour was used to create this waterside walk. Look out for number 27.

Number 27 was the childhood home of Henry "Birdie" Bowers. Bowers, a Merchant seaman, joined Captain Scott's Terra Nova expedition to the South Pole, 1910-1913. He was initially taken on as a storekeeper but so impressed that he was given other tasks. He was 5' 4" tall with red hair and a beak-shaped nose, hence the nickname. He was one of the team of five who set out for the Pole and it was Bower who first spotted the black flag left on the camp by Roald Amundsen's Polar party. On 18 January, they arrived at the Pole to find a tent left by the Amundsen's party at their Polheim camp. Inside was a dated note informing them that Amundsen had reached the Pole on 14 December 1911, beating Scott's team by 35 days. Sadly all Scott's team died in their tent on or about 29 March 1912 (Scott's last diary entry), 148 miles (238 km) from their base camp. The Bower Hills in Antarctica, later renamed The Bower Mountains, were named in his honour.

Further along is the Galt Fountain with steps on either side.

The fountain was erected in memory of the Scottish novelist, entrepreneur, and political and social commentator, John Galt. He was born in 1779 in Irvine and moved with his family to Greenock in 1789. He wrote poetry, drama, short stories and travel writing. He is famous for his Annals of the Parish. He was a friend and travel companion of Lord Byron, about whom he wrote a biography. After years in Canada he returned to Greenock and died in 1939, aged 59. He is buried in the cemetery in Inverkip Street.

Clyde Coastal Path Guidebook

John Galt Fountain Photograph: John MacLeod

Further still, is the red sandstone Sandringham Terrace.

Sandringham Terrace was built in 1900 and stretches from Fox Street to Margaret Street. There are large bay windows at the front and stairs to the upper floors lead from every second entrance. Some are lined with dado borders of tiles depicting scenes of the hills, the Clyde, steamers and yachts. The tiles were produced by the Glasgow Company, James Duncan Ltd, who provided tiles for shops and buildings all over Scotland. There were many off the shelf productions but these were specifically commissioned.

So how did Greenock get its name? Greenock is from the Gaelic word grianaig, the dative case of grianag, 'a sunny place'. I wonder if umbrella sales back this up?

Some think it is Common Brittonic meaning a gravelly or sandy place, which may be an accurate description of the foreshore before the docks and piers were constructed. Others prefer the more romantic suggestion as told in the song, 'The Green Oak Tree'.

"My mither often telt me as she crooned me on her knee,
That Greenock took its name fae the Green Oak Tree."

According to the legend, a green oak tree at the edge of the Clyde at William Street ferry was used by fishermen to tie up their boats. This tends to be dismissed as folklore. The spelling Greenoak was found in two factory accounts dating back to 1717 and the image

Chapter 3. Greenock Esplanade to Victoria Harbour

has been used on banners and badges and carved on public buildings. When we look at the town's coat of arms, however, we see the three chalices of the Shaw Stewarts, a sailing ship and two herrings above the motto, God Speed Greenock. There's just no place for we old romantics.

Arms of Greenock
Heraldry of the World

Greenock developed from a fishing village in the early 17th century into a major port and shipbuilding centre. The shipbuilding industry was founded in 1711 when Scotts Yard began to build fishing boats. In 1774, the River Clyde was deepened, allowing ships to take merchandise directly to Glasgow although some merchants continued to use Greenock Harbour.

Greenock became a centre of industry. Loch Thom was constructed as a reservoir in 1827 and the Kelly and Greenock Cut aqueducts brought the water used to power a paper mill, cotton mills and woollen mills, sugar refineries and shipbuilding. In 1841, Greenock Central railway line opened and provided a fast route to the coast, linking up with the Clyde Steamer Services.

In the 1970s and 1980s, the heavy industries declined and businesses that were bywords in shipbuilding and associated engineering closed. Shipbuilders included Scotts, Browns, William Lithgows and Head the Boat Builder. Marine engineering companies included engine-makers Kincaids, Scotts, Rankine and Blackmore and Lamonts who carried out ship repairs and Hasties associated with steering gear. Yacht builders Adams and McLean and other yards including Cartsburn, Cartsdyke and Klondyke closed during the 1970s and 1980s due to competition from South Korea and Japan.

Clyde Coastal Path Guidebook

Reinvestment and redevelopment of large sections of the town has seen a revival in the local economy. With the development of the Clydeport Container Terminal as an Ocean Terminal for cruise ships, there has been an upsurge in tourism.

Take time out and enjoy the views of the Tail o the Bank.

This was the name given to the anchorage in the Upper Firth of Clyde immediately north of Greenock and Gourock. This area gets its name from the sandbar immediately to its east that marks the entrance to the estuary of the Clyde.

You will come to a yellow pillar with a projecting light and also a connecting light on a pole in nearby Madeira Street.

The pillar may have been moved to this position when the Albert Harbour was excavated. These "leading lights" were part of a network to help ships to navigate on the Clyde. When the two lights were seen in alignment by a ship, it marked a safe anchorage called "The Hole" that provided good holding for anchors.

Decision time! Can you afford NOT to take a detour up to the Lyle Hill to see the most spectacular views of the Clyde on offer? Of course not. (40 minutes uphill climb.) Read on.

Cross the road on to Madeira Street, continue past the site of the now demolished Greenock Academy and at the top of Madeira Street turn right. The road passes Greenock Golf Course on the left before reaching the viewing area on Lyle Hill.

The viewpoint was developed in the 1880s as a means of creating work for the unemployed in the town by the Provost, Abraham Lyle. To the north you can see views of the Holy Loch, Loch Long, the Gareloch and the hills of Argyll. On a clear day, the Isle of Arran can be seen 45 miles to the south.

Chapter 3. Greenock Esplanade to Victoria Harbour

View from the Lyle Hill   Photograph: John MacLeod

On the Lyle Hill, there is an anchor shaped Cross of Lorraine erected in 1946 to honour the Free French sailors who were stationed in Greenock during the occupation of Europe.

Having retraced your steps back down from the Lyle Hill's stunning sights, continue along the Esplanade to the end at Campbell Street. Turn left for toilets and right to continue on the Clyde Coastal Path. On the right, as you turn into Campbell Street, is the Lyle Kirk (Esplanade Building), previous known as the Old West Kirk.

The Old West Kirk was the first Presbyterian church built in Scotland following the Scottish Reformation. It was built by Johne Schawe in 1591, adjacent to the west bank of the West Burn estuary. Shipyards developed between the churchyard and the Clyde. In 1917, Harland and Wolffe drew up development plans that involved expansion over the churchyard and demolition of the Kirk and the cemetery. An agreement was reached to dismantle the church stone by stone and rebuild it on its present site on Campbell Street. The bodies in the cemetery were disinterred and reburied in a mass grave in Greenock central cemetery except the body of Highland Mary. Mary was famous for her relationship with Robert Burns. She was born in Dunoon in 1763, and, aged 5, moved with her family to Campbeltown and finally to Greenock. She was also said to have spent time in Lochranza on the Isle of Arran. Mary was described as tall and fair-haired with blue eyes and spoke English with a strong

Clyde Coastal Path Guidebook

Gaelic accent, hence "Highland Mary". In her early teens she went to Mauchline in Ayrshire to become a nursemaid to Gavin Hamilton, who was landlord, patron and friend of Burns and to whom Burns dedicated the first Kilmarnock Edition of his poems. Burns first saw her in a church in Tarbolton.

By the end of 1785, Jean Armour was pregnant and Burns was the father. Jean Armour and Burns made a legal acknowledgement of an irregular and private marriage. Armour's father objected to this marriage and sought an annulment. The Armour family, including Jean, denied the pregnancy and Jean agreed to move to Paisley. There is a suggestion that Mr Armour's lawyer altered or destroyed the paperwork associated with the marriage. Burns felt aggrieved and deserted and wrote bitterly about Jean Armour's behaviour in the whole affair. He felt that he was entitled to regard himself as a free man.

Burns had a relationship with Highland Mary. It is said they exchanged bibles over a water course and possibly some traditional Scottish matrimonial vows on the banks of the River Ayr, either at Failford, where Mauchline Burn has its confluence, or near Coilsfield. There is a suggestion that Burns and Mary planned to go to Jamaica together. Their brief affair started in April 1786 and their parting was in May 1786. According to Burns she went off to the West Highlands "to arrange matters among her friends for our projected change of life." In the Autumn she sailed to Greenock where they had planned to meet up. Unfortunately, she died, aged 23, of typhus around 20 October 1786 in Greenock before Burns was able to see her again. Doubts have been raised as to whether her death was from typhus or from a complication of childbirth. She was buried in the Old Kirk Cemetery. Burns had dedicated The Highland Lassie, Highland Mary and To Mary in Heaven to her. In 1920 she was reburied in Greenock Central Cemetery under the monument created

Chapter 3. Greenock Esplanade to Victoria Harbour

Greenock   Photograph: Iain R White

by John Mossman in 1842. There are three vertical panels. The upper depicts in bas-relief a weeping maiden, the middle depicts two figures representing Mary and Burns, and the bottom has the following inscription:

"O, Mary, dear departed shade!
Where is thy place of peaceful rest?"

At the top of the road turn left and continue along the A8. On the left is the deep-water port of Ocean Terminal where large cruise ships berth. At Patrick Street turn left and continue down to Container Way and turn right. Carry on until you reach the Mecca Bingo Hall and turn left into Custom House Way. Pass the Waterfront Cinema then go right alongside the water. Go past the Waterfront Leisure Centre and Custom House with the large monument with the clock in front.

The Custom House was built in 1818 by William Burns and is a fine example of Georgian architecture. It was, until 2011, still used by HM Revenue and Customs, one of the last purpose built Custom

Clyde Coastal Path Guidebook

The Custom House, Greenock   Photograph: John MacLeod

Houses still used for its original purpose. A custom house, or customs house, was a building that housed the offices for the government officials who processed the paperwork for the import and export of goods into and out of a country. Customs officials also collected customs duty on imported goods. Typically, the custom house was built in a seaport or in a city on a major river with access to the ocean. Advances in electronic information systems, increase in international trade and air travel changed their role. In 2011, the Revenue moved out and the building now houses the office of the regeneration company, Riverside Inverclyde. They carried out a 4 year project, costing, £4m, to completely renovate the building which had fallen into disrepair. The final work was the refurbishment of the

PG Paper supports the Rotary Club of Gourock, the Clyde Coastal Path and this Guidebook.

Chapter 3. Greenock Esplanade to Victoria Harbour

famous Long Room, where berthing and customs and excise payments where made. Several businesses have leased space in parts of the building refurbished earlier in the project. The Category A listed building celebrates its 200th anniversary in 2018.

Continue until you reach the Beacon Art Centre, turn right and then left and follow the road until you reach the Tail o The Bank restaurant. Turn left and follow the path running parallel to the main road. Near the end of the path, go through the posts on to the pavement and continue until you reach the EE building, built on part of the site of Scotts Yard.

Starting in the early 18th century, Inverclyde rose to become an important shipbuilding area and we are about to pass through the sites of past industrial might stretching along the Clyde to Port Glasgow.

The American colonies built most of the vessels trading with Scotland. Shipbuilding at that time was limited to construction of vessels for herring fishing and other small craft. The Scotts yard was established in 1711 to build such vessels.

Gradually more elaborate vessels were built as the industry developed rapidly in the latter part of the 18th century. Scotts built the first vessel constructed for a non-Scottish owner in 1765. By the end of the 18th century Scotts were regularly building the largest vessels in Scotland as the area now known as Inverclyde became a flourishing port and shipbuilding area. This attracted associated industries such as ropeworks, sail manufacturers, foundries and sawmills that developed in tandem with shipyards. In 1806, Scotts built the first warship, "The Prince of Wales".

Rotary raises money for local causes, including the Beatson Cancer Centre and foodbanks. **Rotary**

Clyde Coastal Path Guidebook

4. Wemyss Bay to Victoria Harbour Muirland Route

Chapter 4. Wemyss Bay to Victoria Harbour

4. Wemyss Bay to Victoria Harbour - Muirland Route

Does the road wind uphill all the way?

Yes, to the very end."

"Uphill"   Christina Rosetti

When you exit Wemyss Bay Station, turn right and continue for 150 yards to just before the bridge over the Kelly Burn. Cross over the road and walk up the hill until the road turns left and a gate ahead opens on to the path leading through mature woodland in the Kelly Glen. The journey to the beginning of the Kelly Cut is about fifty minutes of steady incline. The path runs alongside the lively Kelly Burn as it tumbles over waterfalls down towards the Clyde. In summer the lush cover on the bushes and trees at some parts allows only glimpses of the burn.

The woodland offers a selection of resident and summer visiting birds. All year round there are blackbirds, song thrushes, the aggressively territorial robins, colourful chaffinches, wood pigeons and dunnocks. Don't forget the wren; a small bird that tends to hide in low vegetation. It is quite a singer and, despite its size, its song is surprisingly loud. Its alarm call is a harsh, grating "tick". Its small tail is often cocked. The wren is definitely a bird with attitude. There is a variety of tits, including the long-tailed tit, whose tail is longer than its body. You may also, with luck, catch a glimpse of the tree creeper and the great spotted

Long-tailed Tit   Photograph:David Palmar
photoscot.co.uk

woodpecker, although you may have to settle for the sound of the drumming of the latter.

Spring and summer brings spotted flycatchers, warblers and chiffchaffs. Blackcaps entertain with their melodic warbling high in the canopy.

At one point the path forms a hairpin bend to the left; follow the path. If you choose to turn right and cross the small bridge you will find yourself on the way to Skelmorlie. Further up at the T-junction follow the repeater signs directing to the right. On the left is the Kellybank caravan site. Further up follow the path to the right past the cottage and through the gate. Further uphill, stop, turn back and enjoy the view.

Great Spotted Woodpecker
Photograph: David Palmar
photoscot.co.uk

We can now see Toward Point, the southern extremity of the Cowal peninsula. It is near the village of Toward and is six miles south of Dunoon. The Toward Point Lighthouse, completed in 1812, is one of the eighteen built in Scotland by Robert Stevenson. The location is the southwest extreme point of the Highland Boundary Fault as it passes up the Firth of Clyde..

Six miles north is Dunoon, the main town in the Cowal peninsula, and the birthplace of Mary Campbell, "Highland Mary", of Robert Burns's poem. She was born in Auchanard, Dunoon in 1763.

Chapter 4. Wemyss Bay to Victoria Harbour

Over to the left you can see Rothesay, the principal town on the Isle of Bute. The main town is built around Rothesay Castle that dates back to 13th century. It developed into a tourist town and was very popular with Glaswegians. So much so that they even wrote songs about it, one of which refers to it as "Scotland's Madeira".

The pathway now flattens out a little and becomes more winding, then dips down and once more rises up. At the top of the hill a signpost indicating the beginning of the Kelly Cut directs left towards the Greenock Cut Centre, known as the Cornalees Centre until 2010. Before you continue on your way, recover your breath by taking a last look at Toward Point and the Isle of Bute.

The path, particularly near the beginning can be very muddy and churned up, courtesy of passing cattle and tractor wheels. The path alongside the Kelly Cut flattens and gradually begins its decline.

The Kelly Cut   Photograph: Norman Pettigrew

Clyde Coastal Path Guidebook

The Kelly Cut is a narrow non-navigable channel that was built in 1845 by the engineer, Robert Thom. It is 4 miles (6.5 km) long and is around 500 ft above sea level. The Cut fed water from the Kelly Reservoir on the hill behind Wemyss Bay and the Crawhin Reservoir on Crawhin Hill, near Cornalees, to the Compensation Reservoir at Cornalees. From there it fed the Greenock Cut which supplied water to Greenock for Industrial and domestic use.

Spring and summer are the most productive seasons to see the birds of the uplands. Skylarks, meadow pipits, stonechats and whinchats can be seen. Cuckoos are heard but, as William Wordsworth reported, are notoriously difficult to see.

"Thrice welcome, darling of the spring!
Even yet thou art to me
No bird, but an invisible thing,
A voice, a mystery;"

Despite the warm welcome humans give to its arrival in spring, other birds may not be so joyful. The cuckoo has adopted a far from sociable approach to house building and child rearing. The female cuckoo chooses a nest of another species, especially dunnocks, meadow pipits, pied wagtails and reed warblers, and lays an egg. The cuckoo's egg closely resembles that of the other bird. The cuckoo then removes one of the host's eggs and either drops it out of the nest or eats it. The cuckoo then leaves the host bird to brood and feed her chicks. The baby cuckoo is an ungrateful guest. It has a sensitive depression on its back that it uses to manoeuvre any host egg out of the nest. Across the world there are about 77 species of birds that have adopted this anti-social parasitic brooding habit. Why do they do it? It enables the cuckoo to develop the genetic line. By laying eggs in another nest, the cuckoo can lay many more eggs

Chapter 4. Wemyss Bay to Victoria Harbour

than if she only lays in her own nest. Not only that, it conserves energy normally spent on rearing and feeding the young.

The disappearing curlew can be heard calling. Snipes visit and as they dive at great speed through the air during courtship displays, the wind produces a drumming or bleating sound as it passes through the outer tail feathers.

Birds of prey, mainly buzzards and kestrels, may be encountered and occasionally peregrines, merlins and hen harriers can be spotted.

Loch Thom and the Compensation Reservoirs host gulls, ducks including goosanders and Canada geese.

Also in summer, swallows, house martins and swifts flash by.

Goosander

Photograph:David Palmar
photoscot.co.uk

Follow the path alongside the Cut as it winds its way across the moorland. On your left you will once again see the Clyde and hills in the distance. Towards the end of the path there is a picnic site and pretty soon a gate. Pass through and turn left. Ahead you can see the Greenock Cut Visitor Centre and over to the right, the Ardgowan Fishery with a café.

The Centre, as well as offering welcome toilets, has an interactive exhibition about the Greenock Cut describing the history and workings. It is well worth a visit. The Centre also offers refreshments, a gift shop and information about walks and various other activities

Clyde Coastal Path Guidebook

The Greenock Cut Centre — Photograph: Norman Pettigrew

including talks by Countryside Rangers. It is open daily during the summer months and at weekends during winter.

Across the way is the Ardgowan Fishery Café with the unusual invitation on the door to bring in your dog. It serves hot food and drinks. There are rolls with many fillings, toasties and beefburgers. And whose beefburgers? They are made from the meat from our old friend Mearns T McCaskie in Wemyss Bay. It opens during daylight hours, 365 days of the year. Yes, 365. Yes, Christmas Day. Yes, New Year's Day. And every four years? Yes, 366 days.

After your rest, fuel and enlightenment, head back over to the entrance to the path that leads down and alongside the Greenock Cut.

Take a moment to look at the monument erected, by the Institute of Civil Engineers in 2012, to honour the hydraulic engineer, Robert Thom, who designed this scheme to supply Greenock with water.

Chapter 4. Wemyss Bay to Victoria Harbour

Take the path and after one quarter of a mile pass through a gate and cross the road and through another gate. After a further quarter of a mile there is a concrete Valve House to the left of the path.

The Valve House was also known as a 'waster' and contains a large bucket and chain. This ingenious method controls the water in the Cut. When the water rises in the Cut to flood levels, it flows along the small pipe. The overflow water fills the bucket and the

The Greenock Cut   Photograph: Norman Pettigrew

weight of the extra water pulls the bucket and the chain down. The chain movement opens a hatch in the large pipe. Flood-water pours out of the open hatch and drains away.

When water levels in the Cut fall, water stops flowing along the small pipe and the feed to the bucket stops. A small hole in the bucket allows the water to leak out and the chain rises, pulled by the counterweight. The hatch in the large pipe closes.

The Greenock Cut, like the Kelly Cut, is a non-navigable canal, although longer at 5.5 miles. The Greenock Cut once fed water from Loch Thom to Greenock. Many engineers had attempted to solve the problem of water supply, including James Watt, however it was Robert Thom's scheme that was adopted. Work commenced in 1825 and was completed in 1827. As well as drinking water it supplied

Rhu & Gare Loch from Overton Road   Photograph: Stuart Sharkie

water to power the industries of Greenock. These included mills for paper, wool, flax and flour as well as heavy industries in the east of Greenock.

The Cut runs around Dunrod Hill and Cauldron Hill, at a height of 500 ft. on the way to Overton. It was operational until 1971 when it was replaced by a tunnel. It was designated a Scheduled Monument in 1972.

Continue on the path as it follows the Cut through the moorland.

Look down and enjoy the panoramic view of Greenock and the River Clyde once again, with the Argyll hills in the distance. Greenock stretches a friendly arm around the back of Gourock lying below, hidden by trees on a hill.

The large brown building is Inverclyde Hospital and the smokestacks belong to its laundry. The large green space is Greenock Golf Course and the huge area of trees is the site of

Chapter 4. Wemyss Bay to Victoria Harbour

Greenock Cemetery. The cranes at Ocean Terminal are clearly visible, as are the containers awaiting shipment to Europe.

Further out in the Clyde there is a mound that looks like a sandbank. This is actually the hull of the MV Captayannis, a sugar-carrying vessel, now referred to as the "sugar ship". On 27 January 1974, she was anchored at the Tail o the Bank with a cargo of sugar from Portuguese East Africa. Sugar was one of the major industries of Greenock. She was awaiting high tide to offload her cargo at James Watt sugar terminal for processing at Tate and Lyle Westburn Refinery. The weather deteriorated and a severe storm hit the west coast with winds of more than 60 miles per hour. Captain Theodorakis Ionnis decided to make for the more sheltered waters of the Gareloch.

Also anchored at the Tail o the Bank was a BP Tanker, British Light, recently arrived from Elderslie Dry Dock. Before Captain Ionnis could power up, the storm blew her towards the tanker. They avoided collision but the tanker's anchor chain ripped through the Capayannis's hull as it passed and seawater poured in, overwhelming the pumps. Captain Ionnis tried to ground the ship on the sandbank but the vessel began to heel over to port. This resulted in a loss of all power and the Captayannis's settled port side on the sandbar. All of the crew was rescued without injury by the tug Labrador and the MV Rover of Clyde Marine Service. The ship finally heeled over and settled next morning. The cargo of raw sugar disappeared into the water.

About 8 metres of hull lie below sea level with the starboard side 4 metres above. The structure has been stripped of all its fittings by looters leaving just the steel hull and superstructure and is now inhabited by seabirds and fish. There was some confusion about the owners and insurers and no one accepts responsibility for her removal. Plans to have it blown up were abandoned due to fears that it might cause damage to a nearby bird sanctuary at Ardmore Point.

The grey building between the two cranes was formerly James Watt College, now West College Scotland. The spire over to your left is Westburn Church. It was built in 1840 and the spire dates from 1850. A little further along to the right is the spire of St. George's Church.

The large steeple far over to the right is the Victoria Tower, 245 ft (75 m) tall, a part of the Greenock Municipal buildings. Its architectural style is Italianate and it was completed in 1886. It had an amazing escape in May 1941 during World War Two when a bomb landed just next to it destroying the property that stood there. The gap left behind is known as "Cowan's Corner" in memory of the local shopkeeper who had refused to sell his property when the Municipal Buildings were being constructed, forcing an alteration in the plans. Today "Cowan's Corner" remains vacant and is a landscaped area with seating. The spire a little further to the right again, belongs to Wellpark Mid Kirk.

Walk across the grassy area in front of the path and look down.

The large red building is Greenock prison. Murdieston Dam, used to provide electricity for sugar refineries, is also visible.

Continue back on the path until the end of the Cut and head down the steep hill. Turn left on to the road that bears right as Papermill Road. Keep right on Papermill Road at its gushet with Peat Road. Turn right at Drumfrochar Road and follow it to where it bends sharply left downhill and becomes Baker Street. Continue downhill to a short piece of dual carriageway where it becomes Dellingburn Street. Pass under a bridge to a roundabout. Turn right in to Carnock Street, then left into St Andrew's Street. Turn right along the main road and cross using the pedestrian crossing.

Chapter 4. Wemyss Bay to Victoria Harbour

The PS Waverley under the Erskine Bridge   Photograph: Iain Quinn

Rotary supports youth development nationally via its Young Musician, Young Chef, Young Writer, Youth Speak, to name but four of a range of challenges.

Clyde Coastal Path
Rotary

Clyde Coastal Path Guidebook

5. Victoria Harbour to Woodhall Roundabout

Chapter 5. Victoria Harbour to Woodhall

5. Victoria Harbour to Woodhall Roundabout

Turn left just before the EE building, a Call Centre built on part of the site of Scotts Yard, into Cartsburn Way. Follow this down the side of the EE building and turn right at the bottom of the path and continue alongside the Clyde. Continue until you reach the James Watt Docks with its towering Titan Crane.

Titan Crane at James Watt Dock   Photograph: Peter Smith

This giant 150 ft Titan cantilever crane, now an A listed structure, stands on the south side of the James Watt Dock and weighs in at an impressive 150 tons. It is one of only four left in Scotland, the others being in Finnieston, Whiteinch and Clydebank. It was built during World War One in 1917, by Sir William Arrol & Co Ltd for the Greenock Harbour Trust when there was great competition for material. Arrol & Co. built 40 Titans and of these, 27 were located in Britain. Two non-Arrol Titans were built. One, built by the Motherwell

Clyde Coastal Path Guidebook

Bridge Engineering Company, was exported to Nagasaki, Japan, and is still in use today by Mitsubishi Industries. The other was built by Babcock and Wilcox, Renfrew, and exported to Singapore. Historic Environment Scotland reported in 2014 that only 11 Titans survive around the world. The four surviving Titans in Scotland are all Category A listed.

A lower girder tower supports a roller track on which rotates an asymmetrical cantilever truss jib with a motor room and counter weight on the short end. It is built to lift cargo, including steam locomotives and equipment from engines to boilers, used in building battleships and ocean liners. Titans could be one-man operated and were faster and more efficient than the other cranes at the time.

The construction of the James Watt Dock began on 1 August 1878 and was completed in 1886. It was built to allow Greenock to compete with Glasgow with the aim of attracting transatlantic shipping traffic and establishing Greenock as "one of the greatest and best equipped British seaports". At the time of its development it was believed to be the only dock on the Clyde where vessels of large tonnage could be kept afloat at all states of tide. It was an expensive project that eventually cost about four times its budget. It was felt that the great and rapidly increasing volume of trade passing up the Clyde to Glasgow justified such spending. It was believed that such a facility would allow Greenock to benefit from the larger ships that were being used for trade and passenger traffic but were constrained in their draft to navigate the upper reaches of the Clyde in anything below high tide. This allowed Greenock to enter a period of huge expansion. Together with the staple industries such as sugar refining and shipbuilding the boom in trade led to significant development and growth of the town.

Other docks making up the Greenock harbours include: West Harbour, East India Harbour, Victoria Harbour, Albert Harbour,

Chapter 5. Victoria Harbour to Woodhall

Bollards at James Watt Dock   Photograph: Peter Smith

Princes Pier, West Quay, Customhouse Quay, Garvel Graving Dock and Great Harbour. Some of these harbours and docks no longer operate as functioning harbours and some have been in-filled to expand waterfront development.

Almost two thirds of Britain's tonnage in iron steam ships was produced on the Clyde with many of the ships built and launched at the yards between Greenock and Port Glasgow. Demand for Clyde-built ships reached its peak just before World War One. There has been a steady decline in completions and launches since then. In 1955, 27 new ships were launched from Inverclyde yards but by 1975, the number had dropped to 10. Nowadays, the last remaining yard on the lower Clyde is Fergusons, founded in 1903.

The pedestrian entrance to the James Watt Dock is blocked. Turn back and follow the path to the right into the car park past the Point

Restaurant and continue past the Premier Inn on the right and McDonalds on the left until you reach the roundabout where you turn left. Continue along the main road, East Hamilton Street, for about a mile. On the opposite side of the road, before the James Watt Marina, is the hallowed ground of Greenock Morton FC, Cappielow Park.

Morton, one of the oldest senior Scottish Clubs, was founded in 1874 as Morton FC. In 1994, to celebrate its links with its home town, Greenock, it changed its name to Greenock Morton FC, although it is usually just referred to as Morton.

The reason for the name is unclear. It is generally agreed that it was named after "Morton Terrace", a row of houses next to the original playing field where many of the players lived.

The ground is called Cappielow. The origin of this name is also unclear but is thought to be of Scandinavian origin. The ground has been occupied since 1879 and has a capacity of 11,589 of which 5,741 are seated. The area currently behind the west goal is known as the "Wee Dublin End" because the Irish immigrants to Greenock were housed behind that stand. The north end is referred to as "The Cowshed".

In December 2008, Morton purchased a stand for £50,000 from rivals St Mirren when they moved to a new ground. They also purchased two floodlights to be put at either end of the "Cowshed".

Morton's fortunes have been varied. They won the Scottish Cup in 1922 and have featured in the Scottish Premier League. Unfortunately, they have regularly moved up and down the leagues, but so far have failed to re-enter the premier league. At present they are in the Scottish Championship.

On this side of the road before the entrance to the James Watt Marina is former Sugar Warehouse. This long warehouse, with a

Chapter 5. Victoria Harbour to Woodhall

high first storey, is built of red brick with arches, plaster strips and window margins of yellow brick. The gable ends of the 4 storey blocks have 8 stepped recessed arches.

By the end of the 19th century, 400 ships per year were transporting sugar from Caribbean Holdings to Greenock for reprocessing. There were more than sixteen refineries in Greenock. In 1997, Tate & Lyle ended 150 years of sugar manufacture when it closed down. The building was scheduled as a category A listed building in 1907. The plan is eventually to develop the building for housing.

Cross over the entrance road to the James Watt Dock Marina and continue straight ahead along the main road. About 50 yards before the traffic lights at Port Glasgow Road, you turn left down a slipway and continue until you meet Port Glasgow Road where you turn left towards Inchgreen Drydocks. This is the beginning of Port Glasgow.

Port Glasgow, originally the Port of Glasgow, was once the principal port of the city of Glasgow. It is on the south bank of the Clyde where the river widens and deepens to become the Firth of Clyde. In the days of sail, the town's location on the west flowing estuary in the west of the mainland gave it an advantage in the race to trade with North America.

At that time, goods had to be unloaded at Port Glasgow. These included sugar and, very importantly, tobacco. Glasgow distributed 60% of the UK's tobacco. The goods were loaded on horsedrawn vehicles and transported by road to Glasgow. The wealthy industrialists, particularly the tobacco barons, lobbied for the Clyde to be deepened.

Work began in the 18th century to make the Clyde navigable all the way to the centre of Glasgow. Even today, with its modern technology, such a venture would be regarded as a major undertaking. The work continued throughout the 19th century enabling ships to bypass the town and sail directly to Glasgow. The history of the River Clyde and Glasgow can best be summed up by the statement:

The Clyde made Glasgow and Glasgow made the Clyde.

The completion of the project heralded the death of the harbour trade in Port Glasgow. The gap was filled with shipbuilding that thrives today in the form of Fergusons Shipyard, although on a smaller scale than in the past. Port Glasgow is the second largest of the three Inverclyde towns.

In 1811, when Henry Bell commissioned John and Charles Wood of Port Glasgow to construct his small steamship, the "Comet", he began a revolution in shipping and a new shipbuilding industry in Britain. It weighed 28 tons, was 45 ft (14 m) long, 10 ft (3.0 m) wide and had a 3 horsepower engine.

Henry Bell was born in 1767, at Torphichen Mill, Linlithgow, into a family well known as millwrights, builders and engineers. His training was varied. He was apprenticed to a stonemason in 1780 and three years later was apprenticed to his uncle, a millwright. Later he learned ship modelling in Barrowstounness until 1787 when he went to work with the engineer, James Inglis in Bellshill, to learn more about ship mechanics. After a spell in London, he returned to Glasgow where he worked as a house-carpenter.

Bell was retired from engineering when he engaged with the idea of a steamship while helping his wife in the Helensburgh Baths, a hydropathic establishment. He was very interested in the work of the marine engineer, William Symington, who had built a steamship, the "Charlotte Dundas". In 1801, it had towed two 70 ton barges 19½ miles along the Clyde and Forth canal but was stopped by an edict of the canal owners on the basis of the dubious claim that the

Chapter 5. Victoria Harbour to Woodhall

paddles of the "Charlotte Dundas" were damaging the banks of the canal. Also, he was inspired by the performance of the steam engine, designed by James Watt, used to pump seawater from the Clyde into the hot tubs of the Helensburgh Baths. Bell, however, ignored Watt's reputed comment that a practical marine steam engine was an impossibility.

Bell purchased an engine from John Robertson of Glasgow for £165. He was unable to afford a boiler and needed to seek credit. Financial management was not one of his strengths. He gave David Napier a promissory note for £62 that had to be renewed but was never redeemed. The ship was named after the comet seen in the sky during its construction.

James Watt
Photograph: John MacLeod

On 8 August 1812, the "Comet" made the first commercial steamboat journey in Europe, covering the 24 miles from Broomielaw in Glasgow to Greenock in less than 5 hours against a head wind. Previously this journey would have taken between 10 and 12 hours.

By 1816, a number of competitors was offering services on the Clyde using more advanced vessels. Bell then offered services on the Firth of Forth but was still unable to compete. Realising his boat was too small, he increased its length by 20 ft and, in 1819, he moved to the West Highland route. He ran a service to link Glasgow to Fort William via Oban and the Crinan Canal, the round trip taking 4 days.

In December 1820, she was returning from Fort William when she was caught by the racing tide of the Dorus Mòr off Loch Craignish and was driven on to the rocks. Fortunately all on board escaped unharmed. The boat was lost but the engine was salvaged and continued working, first in a coach building works in Glasgow and then in a brewery in Greenock. In 1862, Robert Napier, the Glasgow engineer, bought it and presented it to the Science museum in London.

Despite his financial losses with the first "Comet", Bell built another. The second "Comet" collided with steamer, "Ayr", off Kempock Point, Gourock. 62 of the 80 people onboard, drowned. The reputation of neither of the crews came out of this tragedy well. The salvaged engine of the second "Comet" is in the Riverside museum, Glasgow. Following this disaster, Bell abandoned his work on steam ship navigation, penniless and in poor health. A number of benevolent individuals began a subscription on his behalf raising over £500. The

The Comet   Photograph: John MacLeod

Chapter 5. Victoria Harbour to Woodhall

trustees of the Clyde granted him an annuity of £100 that was continued to his wife.

Henry Bell died in 1830, aged 62, in Helensburgh and is buried in the Rhu churchyard. In 1883, an obelisk monument to Bell was erected on the Rock of Dunglas, about 2½ miles above Dumbarton. In 1872, a second monument was erected on the seafront at Helensburgh.

A replica of the "Comet" was built in 1962 by the apprentices to commemorate the 150th anniversary of its original launch. In September 1962, the new "Comet" sailed with a party of local people, dressed in period costume, from Greenock to Helensburgh, where they laid a wreath on Henry Bell's memorial. Among the passengers was Bell's great grand-nephew, William Bell. The replica stands today on Shore Street in the centre of Port Glasgow.

Port Glasgow Road road quickly becomes Scott Way. You continue along Scott Way keeping to the left hand pavement. When you come to the junction where Scott Way veers to the right, continue straight on to Crunes Way. Follow this path until you reach the Clyde where you turn right and follow the prepared path alongside the Clyde. When you reach the children's play area, turn right and at the T-junction turn left on to Iron Way. Continue until the road turns right and becomes Lithgow Way. Shortly after turn left. A small spur also called Lithgow Way carries straight on to a cul de sac. Continue until you meet a roundabout.

You will note the sign for B&Q over to the right. In front of the store is a Memorial of Steel Plate to the English painter Sir Stanley Spencer. In 1940, the War Artists' Advisory Committee (WAAC) sent Spencer to Lithgows shipyard to depict civilians at work there. B&Q is in the retail park built on the site of Port Glasgow shipyard. In 1943, James Lithgow complained to the WAAC about Spencer's portrayal of the yard leading to his replacement by Henry Rushbury.

Clyde Coastal Path Guidebook

Spencer's work, Shipping on the Clyde, was given to the Imperial War Museum after the war. The Riverside Museum, Glasgow, now displays Spencer's shipyard paintings in a biannual rotation of works on loan from the Imperial War museum.

Take the pathway to the left that will take you alongside the Clyde. Follow the path as it winds to the right and then left until you reach a second roundabout.

Across the roundabout you can see the Port Glasgow Town Hall. The replica of the "Comet" sits in an ornamental pond in a car park opposite the town hall.

Take the pathway to the left and follow this until you reach a T-junction. Left leads on to Anderson Street, right leads on to Queen Street. Turn right and follow Queen Street to Mirren Shore where you turn right.

Alternatively, turn left on to Anderson Street and carry on around the back of the buildings to Mirren Shore and turn right. This is a rough surfaced car parking and service area that during working hours will be busy with traffic. Continue along until meet end of Queen Street.

From the Mirren Shore you can see two lighthouses. The beams of both their lights marked the centre of the dredged 25 feet deep upper channel between Port Glasgow and Dumbarton, continuing all the way to Glasgow. The offshore lighthouse is the Perch Lighthouse. In 1849, since many ships had run aground or wrecked on the Perch, it was suggested that it be removed. The Clyde Navigation Report in 1860 recommended that instead of removing it they replace it with a cast iron lighthouse on the quay. The West Quay Lighthouse was situated 12 ft higher than the Perch and

Chapter 5. Victoria Harbour to Woodhall

aligned so that both beams of light marked the centre of the new channel.

Follow the route through Coronation Park. Enjoy the view across the Clyde to Helensburgh and the Argyll hills. Follow the path as it curves to right and left, keeping the railings to your left. Eventually it turns right, passes Fergusons Shipyard on the left and brings you up to the main road where you turn left. Before you continue, look at the tall building across the road.

This 8 storey building on the corner of Robert Street and Bay Street, was originally Richardson's sugar refinery in the 1860s. Twenty years, later it was converted for use as a ropeworks. The Port Glasgow Rope and Duct Company, set up by a group of traders in 1736 in a mill where Port Glasgow railway station now stands, sold out to the Gourock Rope Company in 1797. They converted it in 1886. This is now a category A listed building and was converted into loft apartments in 2006/7. To the right there used to be a long, low building which housed the 400 yards long "rope walk". This was used for spinning ropes by means of a very intricate system of tracks, bogeys and machinery. This ran alongside the railway line but was demolished during the 1980s. Housing has now been built on that site.

Continue along the main road past Fergusons Shipyard.

Fergusons is the last remaining shipbuilder on the lower Clyde. It is the only builder of merchant ships on the river, mainly roll-on/roll off ferries primarily for Caledonian MacBrayne. In August 2014, the company went into administration. One month later, Clyde Blowers Capital, an industrial company owned by Jim McColl, purchased the yard for £600,000. Jim, a businessman and entrepreneur, was born in Carmunnock in 1951 and was awarded an OBE in 2001. The shipyard is thriving and has around 400 employees.

Clyde Coastal Path Guidebook

Newark Castle   Photograph: John MacLeod

Follow the road past Fergusons Shipyard until you reach the roundabout. Turn left at the roundabout and follow signs for Newark Castle.

Newark Castle was built in 1478 by George Maxwell. The original castle had a tower house within a walled enclosure. All that remains of the outer defensive wall is from one of the original corner towers. At that time, navigation was made difficult by the narrowing Firth and shifting sandbanks. The location was used to offload seagoing ships and led to the growth of Port Glasgow close to the castle on either side and to the south. When dredging techniques made the Clyde navigable as far as Glasgow, the port became a shipbuilding centre and the castle became surrounded by shipyards. In the late 16th century, Sir Patrick Maxwell inherited the castle. Sir Patrick was a friend of King James VI. He, however, was not "a verray, parfit, gentil knyte". He murdered two members of a rival family and beat his wife

Chapter 5. Victoria Harbour to Woodhall

and locked her up. Lady Margaret failed to get a restraining order against him and after 44 years of marriage, during which she produced 16 children, she fled to Dumbarton.

Pass the castle and continue through Newark Castle Park alongside the river. There is a walkway that runs for about one mile, alternating between concrete and boardwalk, the River Clyde on the left, A8 up on the right. At the end of the walkway, continue through Kelburn Park.

Along the shoreline you will see wooden posts sticking up. These were driven into the mudflats to mark out large timber ponds. In the 19th century, Port Glasgow's and Greenock's shipyards required enormous quantities of cut timber. This was imported from Scandinavia and North America and was stored in these pools to

Timber Ponds at Park Lea   Photograph: John MacLeod

Clyde Coastal Path Guidebook

season them in preparation for their use in construction of wooden ships. When you are enjoying the view of the sea lochs, scraped out by glaciers during the ice ages, and the Argyll hills, you are looking across the Highland Boundary Fault. This is the geological dividing line that separates the Highlands from the Lowlands.

Continue through the park until you reach Parklea. Turn right.

The path does not continue straight on because the area is not safe underfoot for walking.

Parklea is part of the Inner Clyde Nature Reserve, a Site of Special Scientific Interest. It encompasses the intertidal zone of the Clyde Estuary from Clydebank in the east to a line between Helensburgh on the north shore and Greenock on the south shore. The site is important for its extensive saltmarsh habitats and as one of the most northerly of the large west coast estuaries used by migrating birds. The RSPB has managed the Inner Clyde Nature Reserve since 1982.

The gathering of wintering species includes species as diverse as cormorant, eider, goldeneye, oystercatcher, red-breasted merganser, red-throated diver, redshank, curlew, reed bunting and snipe. Gulls and mute and whooper swans also gather. The mute swan is so called because it is the only swan which does not call out in flight.

Turn right and walk through the underpass. On the other side turn right. After 50 yards cross road and go through the tunnel under the railway line-DUCK! Once through to the other side, climb the steps to the pavement and cross over Glasgow Road to the pavement opposite and then turn left up to Woodhall roundabout.

Chapter 5. Victoria Harbour to Woodhall

Oyster Catcher Flock in Flight

Photograph: David Palmar
photoscot.co.uk

Rotary supports national causes:
Kidney Kids Scotland and
Children's Hospice Association
Scotland (CHAS).

Clyde Coastal Path
Rotary

Clyde Coastal Path Guidebook

6. Woodhall Roundabout to Erskine Bridge

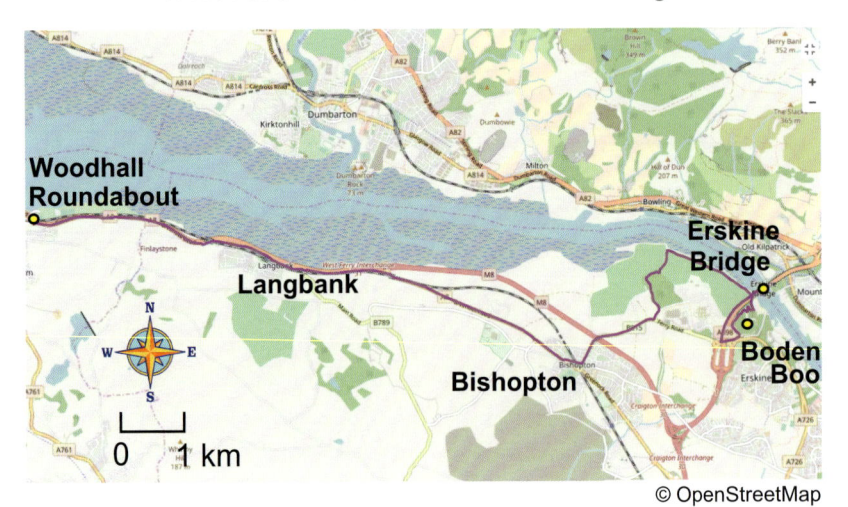

© OpenStreetMap

Chapter 6. Woodhall Roundabout to Erskine

6. Woodhall Roundabout to Erskine Bridge

From Woodhall Roundabout, walk down alongside the A8 motorway, facing the oncoming traffic from which the path is separated by a grass verge. Behind the wall on the right hand side, is the Finlaystone Estate.

The Finlaystone Estate consists of 500 acres of ancient woodland and mature gardens. It also contains Finlaystone House. This mansion was built in 1764 and incorporated the 15th century castle. It has been owned by eight families. The present owner is Gordon MacMillan, the current Chieftain of the Clan MacMillan. Finlaystone was held by the Cunningham family for over 450 years. The Cunninghams were supporters of the Scottish Reformation and hosted the world's first Protestant Reformed communion service by John Knox in 1556. The service was held outdoors under a yew tree. The original tree still stands but its position has been moved.

Robert Burns dined there. He was befriended by James Cunningham, 14th Earl of Glencairn, who acted as his patron and introduced him to many important and influential people of the day, particularly via the Freemasons. Along with his mother he purchased 24 volumes of Burns's poems. When he died in 1791, aged 40, Burns was greatly affected. In a letter to his friend Dr Moore he wrote,

"Glencairn has been the patron from whom all my fame and good fortune took its rise."

And also to Alexander Dalziel,

"God knows what I have suffered, at the loss of my best friend."

In 1794, he wrote a lament to Lord Glencairn and named one of his sons, James Glencairn Burns, after him.

Clyde Coastal Path Guidebook

The estate is operated as a visitor attraction with walks and play areas in the ten acres of gardens.

For a time now, we lose sight of the Clyde. Continue along the path until the railway bridge. The Clyde is once more in view on the left. Pass under the bridge and turn right on to a leafy path. This leads to Main Street, Langbank.

The name, Langbank, is thought to come from "lang bank", "lang" being Scots for long, an apt name as you will see as you progress through the village.

Initially it was a collection of farms that then evolved into a dormitory settlement for Glasgow after the opening of the Glasgow and Greenock Railway in 1841.

Approaching Langbank   Photograph: Iain R White

Langbank is the home to Langbank Parish Church built in 1866 and also St Vincent's College. The college was a minor seminary of the Catholic Church until it closed in 1978, after 17 years. One of its students was the present Archbishop of Glasgow, Philip Tartaglia.

The village is built on the right hand side and the houses have superb views of the Clyde and Dumbarton Rock. Continue through the village, passing the Coast Restaurant, a nice place to have a drink and a comfort stop. Just before the end of Main Street you pass a road on the right leading to an arch bridge. Twenty yards further on, Main Street turns sharply and leads up to another arch bridge.

Chapter 6. Woodhall Roundabout to Erskine

The Clyde Coastal Path, however, continues straight ahead across the road.

Take care crossing Main Street as the views of the traffic in both directions are poor.

The route continues alongside the A8, again facing the oncoming traffic but protected by a barrier and further from the A8 than previously. On the left are fine views of the Clyde and Dumbarton Rock.

Dumbarton Rock is in the town of Dumbarton and its name comes from the Scots Gaelic Dùn Breatann, fort of the Britons. It is also known as Alt Clut, which translates as Rock of the Clyde. It is a volcanic plug that filled the crater of a volcano, active some 350 million years ago. It was the centre of the Kingdom of the Britons that stretched along the River Clyde, north into Stirlingshire and south into Ayrshire. It was also the centre of a Britonnic culture that spoke Old Welsh or Cumbric. Sitting on the Rock is Dumbarton Castle. It has been a royal residence and a fortress with connections from the Vikings to the Scottish Wars of

Path, East of Langbank

Photograph: Iain R White

Independence. Mary Queen of Scots sailed to France from here as a child in 1548.

It is a large rocky peninsula with two peaks. The higher one, 74 m, to the west is more pointed and is called the White Tower Craig after a white tower that stood there in the middle ages. A deep cleft between the two peaks provides a means of access to the upper parts of the rock. Some natural terraces have provided suitable places on which to build. The other peak is about 64 m and is called, the Beak. At its base the rock is 250 m across, east to west, and almost as much north to south. It has wonderful views of the Clyde,

Dumbarton Rock   Photograph: Stuart Sharkie

Loch Lomond and Argyll.

Dumbarton Rock has a long history of occupation and was settled before the town of Dumbarton itself. It enters history in the mid 5th century and early Britonnic kings such as Rydderch Hael helped to secure Christianity in Scotland in the late 6th and early 7th century, and by the mid 7th century was the only Britonnic kingdom in

Chapter 6. Woodhall Roundabout to Erskine

Scotland to survive the attacks by the Angles. In the 9th century, Olaf the White, the Norse king of Dublin, and his brother, Ivaar, laid siege to the Rock and successfully broke through and plundered the kingdom. This led to the end of the Kingdom of Dumbarton and the surviving Britons moved further up river where the new Kingdom of Strathclyde emerged.

Continue until the A8 becomes the M8. The road veers to the right along the route of the old A8. The path widens out and passes through trees. At the end of the path there is a large mound of earth. Just before the mound turn left. The path continues across the road and up to the right. **Take care: traffic**. Delay crossing until nearer the bridge where there is a better path and continue up the hill on to the pavement. This is Hatton Brae leading on to the Old Greenock Road and into Bishopton.

Pause en route up the Brae and turn and take in the view. John Galt, famous for his Annals of the Parish, described the view throughout the climb as one of the best views of the Clyde.

Bishopton was formed in 1840 when the villages of Blackstown and Easter Rossland combined. There is archaeological evidence suggesting agricultural activities took place in this and in the neighbouring Erskine area, around 3000 BCE. There were also some Roman camps in the area, including one at Whitemoss Farm at Bishopton. Around 80 CE a fort had been built that housed the soldiers who patrolled the River Clyde as far as Old Kilpatrick where the Antonine Wall ended, and to guard the Dumbuck crossing. In 1951 and 1954, an archeological excavation revealed a barracks that held the horsemen during the Roman Occupation.

The source of its name is interesting. It took its name from the Bishopton House, home of the famous Brisbane family. They moved to Largs in 1770 where their son, Thomas, was born in 1773 in

Clyde Coastal Path Guidebook

Brisbane House. He became the governor of the colony of New South Wales where they named the state capital, Brisbane, after him. This road passes by Bishopton House on the left, which in 1948 became a convent for the Catholic nuns known as the Sisters of the Good Shepherd. A home for girls, St. Euphrasia, a school, St Gerard's and a church were also added. In 1985, the house was renamed the Good Shepherd Centre, and provides a secure, close support unit for vulnerable young people. It also houses the Cora Foundation, an Agency of the Catholic Bishops' Conference of Scotland, the body that provides support for the Good Shepherd Centre.

Once a farming community, Bishopton is now a commuting village for those who work in Glasgow and Paisley.

Follow Old Greenock Road for a couple of miles until you reach Chestnut Roundabout.

At Chestnut Roundabout you will see a sign to a new housing development to the south of the village. This is the site of a former World War Two Royal Ordinance Factory manufacturing propellants and explosives for large calibre guns. The site covered 2,000 acres and contained 1,500 buildings, 75 miles of narrow gauge railway and 25 miles of standard gauge line. At full production, 25,000 people were employed over three shifts.

The buildings involved in the production and processing of explosive materials were of light construction and in the event of an explosion would disintegrate. They were protected on all sides by large earth mounds called bunds. Some other buildings, for example, ones where propellants were extruded or stored, were also bunded. Most others were of strong construction. The buildings were laid out in a pattern with distances between determined by explosive load

Chapter 6. Woodhall Roundabout to Erskine

and type. Many were of an industrial type found in any chemical factory.

The factory also generated its own electricity. This produced steam that was used to heat the factory by a system of steam distribution pipes and also used in some processes.

Carry on straight through to the junction where Old Greenock Road meets the A8. Diagonally opposite is the Bishopton Inn, ideal for a break to refuel. Turn left into Old Greenock Road and after 200-300 yards turn left at the junction on to Ferry Road / A815. Follow this road as it curves over the M8. Pass Golf Road and past the monument to Lord Blantyre in the field.

The 80 ft monument, designed by William Burn, was constructed in the obelisk style around 1825, to commemorate the bravery of Robert Walter Stuart, the 11th Lord Blantyre, who built and lived at Erskine House, now Mar Hall. He was a Major General in the British Army during the Napoleonic Wars with the Duke of Wellington. Unfortunately he was accidentally killed in 1830 in Brussels by a stray bullet during a street fight. The monument became a Category B listed building in June 1980.

Cross over North Porteous Road that leads to Erskine Home Farm. At the entrance to Mar Hall, turn left and continue for 300 yards and turn left into a small car park. This is the entrance to the Big Wood. There are repeater signs on the fence indicating the Clyde Coastal Path.

Follow the path on the left side running alongside a farm field, separated by a ditch, some trees and a fence. Parts of the path throughout the Big Wood can be muddy and churned up. The path alters with the season. In autumn, it is a beautiful carpet of red and golden leaves.

Clyde Coastal Path Guidebook

Listen and look out for a wide range of woodland birds. The wood can be a noisy place when the crows with the short guttural "Kaa" repeated 3 or 4 times in quick succession compete with the "Krrro, Krrro, Krrro" of the raven.

The path can meander a little and it requires stepping over some slim, fallen trees. At a farm gate with the green bench in front, the path veers to the right leading further into the wood. A repeater sign guides the way. Now the path narrows with trees on both sides. Keep on the path as it veers right, maintaining the high route. As you walk along, you can see the fairways of the Erskine Golf Course and now, season permitting, catch glimpses of the Clyde with distant hills.

Now you will come to a post in the middle of a path leading to the left with a repeater sign directing you down towards the Clyde. This path is steep at the beginning and if muddy, particularly when fallen leaves are covering the roots of trees, can be slippery. The path carries on between the fairways of the Erskine and Mar Hall Golf Courses down to the south bank of the River Clyde where you turn right. Looking ahead, you can now see the imposing form of the Erskine Bridge. On the left, a variety of leisure and commercial craft, including The Waverley, sail up and down the Clyde. There are plenty of opportunities for bird watching. Up to the right is Mar Hall.

Mar Hall is a 5-star hotel and golf resort. It is situated in Erskine House, a Baronial Mansion in style, formerly Erskine Hospital and now a category A listed building. The Lords Blantyre took over ownership of the Erskine Estate and House in the early 18th century. In 1828, Major-General Robert Walter Stuart, 11th Lord Blantyre, commissioned the present house at a cost of £50,000. The architect was Sir Robert Smirkie who also designed the British museum. The building lay empty when the peerage of the Lords Blantyre ended in 1900. In 1916, it was renovated and opened as the Princess Louise

Chapter 6. Woodhall Roundabout to Erskine

Scottish Hospital for Limbless Sailors and Soldiers and shortened later to Erskine Hospital. It was sold to fund the replacement building, Erskine Home, which opened in 2000.

In 2004, the old Erskine Hospital building was converted into a 5-star hotel. Its official name is the Earl of Mar Hotel, after a previous owner of the Erskine Estate, although is generally referred to as Mar Hall.

Pass under the Erskine Bridge and follow the path leading to Boden Boo.

Boden Boo is a woodland area with about 2 miles of informal trails and picnic areas and a beach. The Forestry Commission is responsible for this area. This unusual name is thought to mean bow

Erskine Bridge on a Wet Day   Photograph: Peter Smith

shaped, and refers to a local hill or island. Old maps show a nearby island named Bodinbo, and later Bottombow.

Clyde Coastal Path Guidebook

Pass under the bridge. Further along the path on the right there is a repeater sign on a wooden refuse bin indicating the Clyde Coastal Path.

If you are in need of some refreshment or food, or a good night's sleep, you can carry straight on to the Erskine Bridge Hotel. Continue until you reach Boden Boo car park. Cross the car park to the walk and cycle path to the left. Follow the path to a path triangle where you should bear left and left again. Continue until the second junction and bear right. The path will deliver you to a minor public road where you turn left. This will lead you to the entrance of the Erskine Bridge Hotel.

If continuing on the main Clyde Coastal Path, turn first right after the sign and follow the route uphill through the Boden Boo woodland. The route is a winding climb and descent with many junctions with helpful repeaters advising right turns. There are five right turns. The first right turn takes you further into the woods. You can now hear the sounds of traffic on the Erskine Bridge and can catch sight of the bridge through the trees. Right at the next junction, right again at the T-junction and take the right arm at the Y-junction.

The path now descends to the other side of the woods. At the Y-junction, pause. Ahead on a slim tree in the middle of some bushes a repeater sign points straight ahead: veer right and then right again at the next T-junction. Follow the path over the small section of duckboard and turn right on to the main road.

Stay on the pavement and follow it past the roundabout. Just before the bridge there is the entrance to the eastern route over the bridge. Sometimes during maintenance work the western access is closed. On those occasions, cross over the eastern path and at the north side turn right and follow the path under the bridge to join the Coastal Path on the western side. Pass under the bridge and come to the

Chapter 6. Woodhall Roundabout to Erskine

western access to bridge. Turn right and begin the journey over the Clyde.

Now may be the time for a comfort break and some refreshment before you tackle the bridge. If so, continue on the pavement until it leads round to the entrance to the car park of Caulder's Garden Centre and the delights of the Vanishing Willows tearoom.

The Path through Boden Boo

Photograph: Iain R White

Clyde Coastal Path Guidebook

7. Erskine Bridge to Hardgate

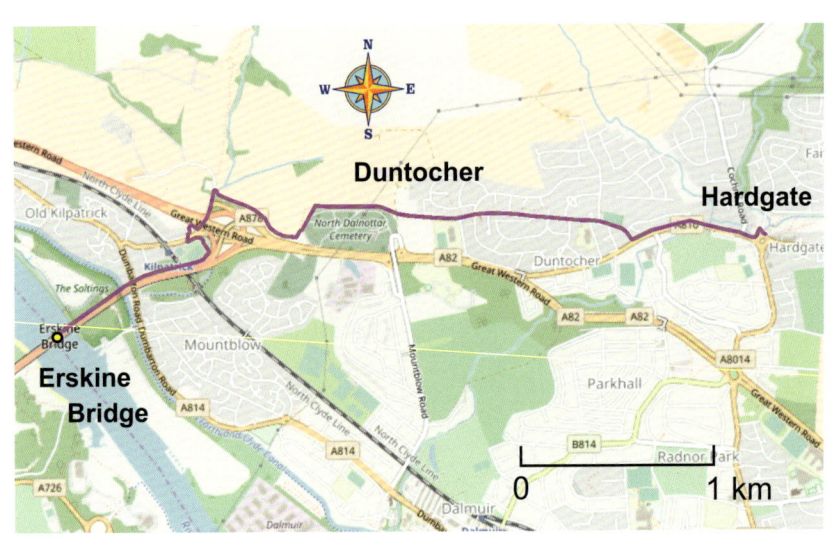

Chapter 7. Erskine Bridge to Hardgate

7. Erskine Bridge to Hardgate

Tighten your haversack, gird your loins and take a deep breath, because you are now about to hike over the Erskine Bridge. It's a bigger climb than it looks. However, you will have an excuse to rest en route when you stop to enjoy the views up and down the Clyde.

The Erskine Bridge   Photograph: Peter Smith

The Erskine Bridge, A898, spans the River Clyde, and connects Renfrewshire in the south with West Dunbartonshire in the north. HRH Princess Anne officially opened the bridge on 2 July 1971.

It is a cable-stayed box girder bridge and is the only bridge in Scotland with single cables over central main supports. It was designed by William Brown, a structural engineer and bridge builder, who specialised in suspension bridges.

The total length of the bridge, including approaches, is 4336.8 ft (1,321.87 m) and it has a clearance of 148 ft (48 m). The weight of the steel is 11,700 tonnes and 1,250 miles of galvanised wire were

Clyde Coastal Path Guidebook

used during construction. The deck and piers have been designed to flex with temperature changes. The total cost, including approaches, was £10.5 million. It was a toll bridge until 1 March 2006.

Despite the fact that the bridge is set at a high level to allow the passage of ships beneath, there was an incident on 4 August 1996 involving the Texaco Captain platform. The oilrig, constructed upstream at Clydebank, was being towed down the river Clyde when it collided with the underside of the road deck, damaging the bridge.

Unfortunately, the bridge is notorious for suicides. It has been estimated that more than fifteen persons per year died by suicide, jumping from the bridge. A lot of work has gone into building preventative barriers. The Samaritans have placed signs at each path leading on to the bridge. There are also four public telephone boxes situated on the twin footpaths running adjacent to the roadway on either side of the river.

On a lighter note, there have been two known births on the bridge. Oliver Erskine Edwards was born on 19 September 1990 and delivered by an unknown police dog handler, and Kiera Sarah-Marie McFetteridge on 18th January 2011 gave birth in an ambulance.

If you have crossed the bridge by the west footpath, bear left behind the telephone box as you leave the bridge. Go through the bollards and follow the path round the north end of the football pitch. If you have crossed by the east footpath, do a right U-turn round the end of the crash barrier, pass under the bridge and turn up right and continue to the path leading round the football pitch to a small bridge. Fifty yards ahead is a bowling green. Cross over the bridge. There is no footpath on the bridge so look out for traffic that fortunately tends to be light. Turn right down Mount Pleasant Drive and at the bottom of the hill turn left along the footpath beside Station Road

Chapter 7. Erskine Bridge to Hardgate

and continue through the underpass under the A82. Carry on beyond the underpass and north past the slip road to Glasgow until the track on right leading through Filshie's farm. Turn right and continue up the farm track following the fence on your right. The path tends to be muddy and rutted.

The Kilpatrick Hills from the Path   Photograph: Stuart Sharkie

The low building on the left as you are nearing the top is the remains of an old piggery. This has been used as a canvas for local graffiti artists. Some made the journey to advertise their allegiance during the Scottish referendum campaign in 2014. There's devotion for you.

Turn left at the end of the field and continue until you reach the kissing gate. Pass through this gate and follow the path uphill alongside Dalnottar Cemetery to the top where you will turn right.

This path was repaired and resurfaced by the West Dunbartonshire Community Payback Scheme.

Clyde Coastal Path Guidebook

At the top, before turning right, take a few steps to the gate on your left and enjoy a view of the iconic Erskine Bridge and the River Clyde.

You are now about to embark on a journey that will take you through the villages of Duntocher, Hardgate and Faifley. There is evidence on this route of Roman occupation and also prehistoric habitation. A plentiful supply of water from the Kilpatrick Hills, via the Humphrey and Cochno Burns, made the land attractive to farmers and also drove the textile industry. Like the towns visited in Inverclyde, these three villages were irrevocably changed by the Industrial Revolution and have suffered the ravages of post-industrial Scotland.

Tree at Dalnottar Cemetery
Photograph: Iain R White

Continue along the path that will run more or less straight to the heart of Duntocher.

"Salve, O Wayfarer", you are now walking in the footsteps of the Roman legionnaires along the northernmost frontier of the Roman Empire, Antonine's Wall. This was named after Antoninus Pius (86-161 CE), who was emperor of Rome from 138-161 CE.

The construction began in 142 CE and it took about 12 years to complete. The wall was a turf and stone fortification and it ran from Carriden near Bo'ness on the Firth of Forth to Old Kilpatrick in West Dunbartonshire on the Firth of Clyde. It was 39 miles (63 km) long, 10 ft (3 m) high and 16 ft (5 m) wide. Security was bolstered by a deep ditch on the northern side and was protected by forts every

Chapter 7. Erskine Bridge to Hardgate

2 miles (3.3 km) with small fortlets between. There were about 17 fortlets constructed and 6000-7000 men stationed along the wall. On the southern side was a road known as the Military Way that was built to facilitate movement of troops bearing supplies, and the carrying of commands and news.

During construction, the soldiers lived in leather tents and wooden huts inside temporary camps. Some were legionnaires but the majority were auxiliary troops mainly drawn from the Roman military system from across the Empire, often by force. Many were from Syria. The soldiers commemorated the construction of the wall and their struggles with the Caledonians in decorative slabs, 20 of which have survived. The slabs, along with monumental sculpture and other Roman artefacts recovered, are on display in the Hunterian Museum, Glasgow.

The Wall was abandoned 8 years after completion and the garrisons relocated to Hadrian's Wall. In 208 CE, the Emperor Septimus Severus re-established the legions on the Wall and ordered repairs. This led to the Wall sometimes being referred to as the Severan Wall by later historians. Despite his age, 70, Severus led the troops into the country to complete the conquest of Britain. The occupation was ended a few years later and was never again fortified. It is reported that the ambushes by the Caledonians, who hung unseen on the flanks and rear of Severus's army, the coldness of the climate and the severity of a winter march across the hills and morasses of Scotland cost the Romans over 50,000 men.

What was life like on the Wall?

Commanding officers had their wives and children with them. Ordinary soldiers were not allowed to marry but many had unofficial wives and children in civilian settlements outside the fort. A settlement was referred to as a vicus. The commanding officers and

Clyde Coastal Path Guidebook

their families, including children, lived privileged lives in the most lavish quarters of the fort, the praetorium. They had heated rooms, bathing facilities, slaves' quarters and a private dining room. Oh, the trials and tribulations of leadership.

Keep on the path running alongside Dalnottar Cemetery. Cross over Carleith Road and continue on the wall, now covered in red blaes.

The Opening of the Thomas Wood Path

This part of the path, leading to Beeches Road, is called the Thomas Wood Path. It was constructed by the West Dunbartonshire Community Payback Scheme and was named after the supervisor, a well-known local man, Thomas Wood. Sadly Thomas died suddenly just days before the official opening of the path by local

Chapter 7. Erskine Bridge to Hardgate

MSP, Gil Paterson. Thomas's fiancée and sister attended and assisted Gil to cut the tape.

The team working on the path was able to find and clear the dense undergrowth from the side of the path to reveal a famous local and much loved landmark, the Summer Stone. This was a regular meeting place to commune in various ways and enjoy the view of the Clyde.

At the end of the path, continue on to Beeches Road. The Wall swept down along the route of Beeches Road. The need for housing unfortunately led to the sacrifice of large parts of the wall.

As you march down Beeches Road in your toga and sandals, I am sure you are asking, "Just who was Titus Aurelius Fulvus Boionius Arrius Antoninus Pius, and what sort of man was he?" Incidentally, on his accession, his name became, "Imperator Caesar Titus Aelius Hadrianus Antoninus Augustus Pontifex Maximus". He clearly loved a snappy name. It is thought the main reason for the title Pius was that he persuaded the Senate to deify Hadrian, he of the 80 mile long wall down south, whom he succeeded. That's typical of the Romans. They did not do the trivial: the making of knights and baronets. They made Gods.

Surprisingly, in all his 75 years, 23 of which he was Emperor, he never once set foot outside of Italy. Although his reign was relatively peaceful, there were several military disturbances throughout the Empire. The unrest in Britannia led to the construction of the Wall. He was unique among emperors in that he dealt with crises and provincial matters through his governors or through imperial letters to the cities.

Records describe him as a modest, intelligent man. He drained his own personal treasury to assist distressed provinces and cities and everywhere exercised rigid economy, hence his nickname, "cummin splitter". He was married to Faustina with whom he had 4 children, 2 boys and 2 girls. All the children, apart from Faustina the Younger, died before Antoninus was elevated to Emperor. Unfortunately, his wife, Faustina, became renowned for her marital infidelity. Perhaps that is why he never left Italy. Despite this, they remained married until her death in 140 CE. In 141 CE, Antoninus built a temple in the Forum and dedicated it to his now deified wife. After his death, he was also deified and the temple was re-dedicated to them both.

At the end of Beeches Road is the main street of Duntocher, Dumbarton Road.

It is thought that the name, Duntocher, is derived from the Gaelic for "fort on the causeway", Dùn Tòchair. There is evidence of life from prehistoric times around Duntocher. A stone age axe was found in nearby Carleith and cup and ring markings on rocks a mile or so to the north are thought to be around 5,000 years old. It is suggested that it began as a farming community along the line of the Roman wall which after leaving Goldenhill crosses the Duntocher burn at the east end of the village before making its way to Old Kilpatrick.

CHOICE ALERT!

Continue on Dumbarton Road to Hardgate or cross over the road and through the gates. Don't turn down the chance to see more things Roman by following this short diversion. Cross the road and pass through the gates into Duntocher Village Green.

Just inside the Green is a history board recounting how this site was originally a scrapyard and lay unused for 15 years. The West Dunbartonshire Council received a grant from the then Scottish Executive and created this Green covering 0.4 hectares. It offers a diverse range of habitat for wildlife, including plants.

Chapter 7. Erskine Bridge to Hardgate

As well as watching robins boldly popping in and out of hedgerows listen out for the song thrush. How do you know it's a song thrush and not another bird, say for example, a mistle thrush? Easy, the song thrush thinks its song is so good it sings it twice, or three times and when it's really on a roll, four times. You may also catch site of a fox or a shy, retreating roe deer.

Once inside the gate, turn immediately left and follow the path as it curves down to the right leading to a footbridge. Pause on the footbridge and look up at the stone bridge to the left.

The bridge, referred to as the "Roman Bridge", spans the Duntocher Burn. The burn rises among the Kilpatrick hills from the Cochno burn and other headwaters and collects in Duntocher before running two and one half miles to the River Clyde. Along the stretch of the burn it is known as the Cochno, Duntocher or Dalmuir Burn.

Despite the title "Roman", the bridge is a much more modern structure, built in the eighteenth century and rebuilt in 1943 due to damage in the World War Two. It is likely, however, that a bridge was located around this site in Roman times given that the Roman Wall crossed the burn at this point. In the west parapet, there is a stone in the style of a Roman distance slab. This has a Latin inscription recording the repair of the bridge in 1772 by Lord Blantyre. There is also a note in English that it was damaged in 1941 during the Clydebank Blitz and repaired in 1943.

Once over the footbridge, the path turns left then uphill. At the top, cross over the road and enter through the gates of Golden Hill Park, originally known as Gowdenhill.

On the right on the west slope of Goldenhill, a Roman bathhouse was discovered near the Duntocher War Memorial just north of the Trinity Church. Several rows of the pillars and passages were uncovered along with reddish tiles in 7 different sizes. A carved female figure, now in Glasgow University's Hunterian Museum, was also discovered.

The World War One memorial that had been erected in 1921 was destroyed in 1941 and replaced by the current memorial in 1951. The Trinity Church, built in 1836, met the same fate and was rebuilt in 1952.

Follow the path uphill round the hairpin-bend to the right until you come to the railed enclosure.

This contains a visible short length of the rampart's stone base.

Carry on uphill, past the enclosure and at the junction follow the path as it turns sharply to the left and continues to the summit of Goldenhill.

Here at the top of the hill, a small fort and fortlet have been located and excavated. West Dunbartonshire Council has begun to mow grass strategically on the site to highlight the lines of the fort, fortlet and wall ramparts.

Continue on the path as it descends towards Hardgate Cross. Exit the gate and turn left and continue along the pavement until you find a suitable place to cross over on to the pavement on the other side. Turn right and make your way to the roundabout.

Well, Wayfarer, it is time to say, "Valete", to things Roman and move on into the 18th century and meet an entrepreneur extraordinaire.

End Polio Now Campaign. Rotary has been a major contributor internationally both in the donation of skills and financially, backed up by the Bill and Melinda Gates Foundation matched grants.

Rotary

Chapter 7. Erskine Bridge to Hardgate

A Quiet Path Just North of the Busy A82   Photograph: Iain R White

Path, Just West of Dalnottar Cemetery   Photograph: Iain R White

Clyde Coastal Path Guidebook

8. Hardgate to the Stockiemuir Road

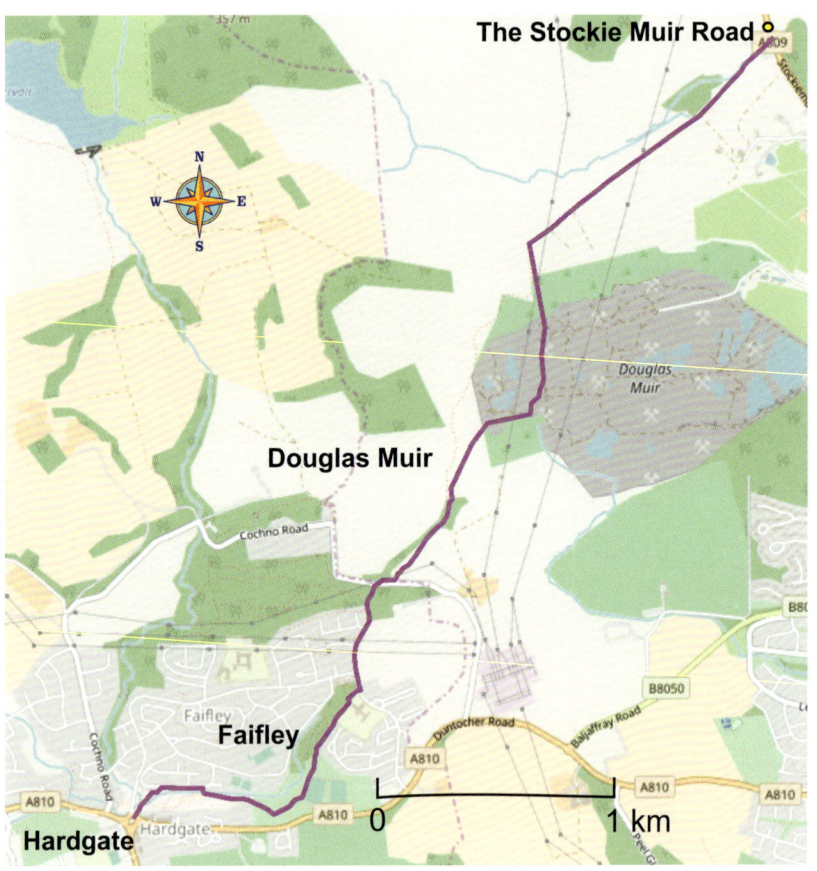

Chapter 8. Hardgate to Stockiemuir Road

8. Hardgate to the Stockiemuir Road

Whether you have come straight from Beeches Road and have walked along Dumbarton Road or you have taken the route through Duntocher Village Green and Goldenhill Park, you are now approaching the roundabout that used to be Hardgate Cross.

The original village of Hardgate or "the Hardgate", was formed around the old turnpike road from Dumbarton to Stirling or Glasgow to the east of Duntocher village. It is possible that its name derived from the "hard gait" or road that passes through a rocky area known as Hardgate Knowes, as the road leaves the village to the east. The original north arm of the road went through the hamlet of Faifley to the farms and estates on the south side of the Kilpatrick Hills. Clydebank was expanded after World War Two and a roundabout was built at the Cross.

When you reach the roundabout, follow the fence until it allows you to cross over to the pavement on the other side and veer right towards the small car park. Pass through the car park and follow the path to the left of Drummond Funeral Directors Ltd, leading into Faifley.

The name Faifley derives from the Scots Gaelic Fionn-Bhealach, that translates as white mountain pass. Over the years, in documents concerning transfers of land, it was recorded as, Fimbalach in 1227, Ferchlay in 1587 and in 1594, Fachla.

Cross the Cochno Burn via the bridge and immediately turn right and follow the diagonal path that runs behind the Faifley Community Seventh-day Adventist Church up to Craigs Avenue. Now it is time to introduce you to William Dunn.

Clyde Coastal Path Guidebook

William Dunn was an entrepreneur, born in 1770, in Gartclash, Kirkintilloch, who went on to become a major influence in the life of the three villages. Before he reached 18, he was orphaned and, responsible for the care of four brothers and a sister. He trained as a cotton spinner in Glasgow and then spent four years learning iron turning and machine making. Around 1800, having accumulated a few hundred pounds, he started his own business manufacturing machinery in High John Street, Glasgow. In 1808, he bought the Duntocher Mill and over the next 23 years acquired Faifley Mill, Dalnottar Ironworks and built Hardgate Mill. He came to own much of the surrounding land and eventually employed nearly 2000 people in cotton manufacturing, agriculture and mining. By 1835, 1400 were employed in the mills alone. All this enterprise was powered by the Duntocher Burn. William Dunn died, aged 78, at Mountblow in 1849. He was buried in the Glasgow Necropolis with a monument designed by John Thomas Rochead. He left property worth £500,000.

Duntocher Mill, like Dunn's other mills, ran into trouble in the 1860s when supplies of raw cotton dried up during the American Civil War. It continued under different owners making yarn and thread until 1920.

In 1808, the population of Duntocher was 200 and rose dramatically with the demand for labour in Dunn's operation. Many of the incomers were from the Highlands following the clearances and a large contingent came from Ireland, driven by the potato famine. Both sides of the main street became lined by houses, shops of all kinds and several pubs. With the closure of the mills in the late 19th century and early 20th century, many of the inhabitants of Duntocher found work in the shipyards and factories of Clydebank.

There is evidence of early settlements in the area. A Neolithic burial site has been discovered at Knappes Farm, Drumry, at the Boulevard. Cup and ring marks have been found on exposed rocks

Chapter 8. Hardgate to Stockiemuir Road

at Cochno and a burial chamber at Cairnhouse above the Cochno Loch.

In 1887, Rev James Harvey of Duntocher, discovered a huge slab of rock measuring 42 ft by 26 ft, on farmland near what is now the Faifley housing estate. It is covered by more than 90 indentations, or "cups", and grooved spirals, along with a ringed cross and a pair of four-toed feet. This has been named The Cochno Stone. It displays what are regarded as the finest examples of Bronze Age "cup and ring" carvings in Europe and are around 5,000 years old. These rock carved symbols are found mainly in Scotland and North of England. Similar carvings have been found in Hawaii, India and Africa. In Scotland, they tended to be found along the west coast near seas or rivers, often close to copper mines.

Cup & Ring Markings, Cochno
Courtesy of West Dunbartonshire Council Libraries & Cultural Services

The carvings generally take the form of:

• circular hollows cut into rock surfaces ("cupmarks"), occurring singly or in groups

• a cupmark surrounded by a circular channel ("cup and ring mark"), occurring with single or multiple rings

• complex designs involving cups, cup and rings, with grooved channels linking or enclosing parts of the design.

Clyde Coastal Path Guidebook

What are they? There are many theories ranging from maps, religious or ritual purposes, astronomical, a portal of life and death and art. It has been observed that the sites appear to have been chosen so as to give uninterrupted views over the surrounding countryside.

Cup and Ring Marks
Photograph: Iain R White

The Cochno Stone has been designated as a scheduled monument. Unfortunately, due to vandals' attempts to contribute more modern additions to the stone, it has been covered by vegetation and surrounded by trees. Gil Paterson, local MSP, is very supportive of the idea that it should be uncovered and put on display in a purpose-built building on site. That is a motion worth voting for.

Until the arrival of William Dunn and the development of the cotton industry, Hardgate was mainly associated with farming. More houses were built and it became a thriving area for small businesses. With the demise of the cotton industry and the development and growth of Clydebank, Hardgate changed from a small traditional country village into a large residential suburb of Clydebank.

Turn right into Craigs Avenue and follow the road past elderly lockups on the right. Pass the footbridge on the right and continue on the Avenue to just before where Craigs Avenue turns left. Turn right at signposts. Pass between concrete blocks and turn left at junction. Pass through barrier. This path has been built on top of the bricks and masonry from the demolition of the Singer Sewing Machine Company building in Clydebank. Continue on this path for at least ¼ mile until you reach a T-junction at which you turn left.

Chapter 8. Hardgate to Stockiemuir Road

You are now going through Faifley Knowes. Continue until you come to a Y-junction at which take the right arm. Follow the path to another path ahead that is uphill and has some broad steps; a not insignificant climb. At the Y-junction near top of the stairs stay left. The path is bordered on both sides by bushes and trees. Further on, there are playing fields on your right. Continue straight on as directed by the signpost. Remain on the path as it curves right and continue straight ahead at next junction.

This whole area is within the reach of the lava flows from local volcanoes. The name Craigs used in street names is derived from Scots Gaelic. Creag translates as a rock or a rock face and refers to areas of basalt rock, an igneous rock, formed by the edge of the flow of the lava. You can see rocks protruding from the earth and you will be aware of standing at points on the edge of a basalt cliff.

After a steady climb, you will come to a grass "roundabout" surrounded by fencing. Go straight ahead and continue on the path alongside a fence with a grassy area and St Joseph's Primary School. At the junction with Faifley Road, turn left. At the bottom of the hill, Faifley Road turns left. Do not follow it. Instead, cross over on to Douglas Muir Road and continue uphill on the pavement on the left. Shortly after joining Douglas Muir Road across on the other side is a small area built on a slope, "Arthur's Brae", that leads you around a series of picture boards describing the Douglas Muir Wildlife Trail. Continue uphill, cross over the entrance to Swallow Road on the left, unmarked, and almost at the top, cross over the entrance to Field Road on the left and continue until you reach four concrete bollards and join the red blaes path. Follow this path first along the level, across three burns and then up the steep hill through Achadh na Creag Wood until you reach the Cochno Road.

Before we leave Faifley, it is worth a pause to think about how this quiet hamlet changed over the years as industrialisation marched

Clyde Coastal Path Guidebook

into the area. Faifley had its own Waulkmill in 1643 and later a Dye Works. William Dunn purchased Faifley spinning company in 1811 and eventually had four mills on the Burn. He introduced the first steam engine in Faifley in 1836. Three of the four mills closed during the American Civil War and the fourth, the Faifley Mill, changed use to a factory making furniture. After World War Two, it was occupied by a small company making and repairing dairy and refrigeration equipment and then latterly by a bakers. Finally it closed in 1991 when it was demolished to make way for housing.

In 1949, Faifley was annexed under the Clydebank Extension Act and work began in 1953 on a new housing scheme. Eventually the housing scheme had a population of 9,000. The housing stock suffered from high density building of poor construction methods until major rebuilding took place leading to replacement by better quality housing of lower density, reducing the population to nearer 4,000.

Sadly, over a comparatively short time, this historic community has lost its identity and has been absorbed into its neighbour, Hardgate, and its name taken by a large housing estate. The local people are very proud of Faifley and its long history.

Turn right on to Cochno Road and after about fifty feet turn left up on to the red blaes path. Later on, sections of the path are exposed to weather and the hooves of heavy cattle and can be churned up and muddy and necessitate protective footwear and clothing. The sections of the path with the red blaes cover were constructed by the West Dunbartonshire Community Payback Scheme. Keep to the left under the pylons. Further up, the burn with surrounding scrub woodland is apparent on the left. At the path junction, turn left with a wood now close to your right. Continue on the path until you reach the kissing gate.

Chapter 8. Hardgate to Stockiemuir Road

The path from Cochno Road is the early part of the Bankie Trail. Until the building of the Faifley housing scheme the path started at the Hardgate Mill and followed the burn up to Whitehill Farm. It continued north across the farm on to the Douglas Muir leading eventually to the Craigton Bleach Works and further north to the mills in Milngavie. Workers in the Bleach Works and mills would make their way back and forward along this trail everyday.

In March 1941, during World War Two, Clydebank suffered greatly from the bombing by the German Luftwaffe. Many people stood on the elevated sites and watched the terrible fires and destruction of their homes. One third of houses were destroyed and another one third badly damaged.

Whitehill Farm Path
Photograph: Community Payback Team

   Pass through the gate and turn right immediately and carry on up the gently sloping path running alongside a fence to the trees at the top. Turn left and follow the path through the wooded area bounded on both sides by a fence. Keep out, cows!

Clyde Coastal Path Guidebook

It is worth a minute to stop and look at the panoramic views. On the skyline, looking south, between the tall buildings you can see the Titan Crane of Clydebank. It is also possible to see planes land and taxi along the runways at Glasgow Airport.

Look out for startled roe deer as they take flight and leap and bound over the moorland. You can track their route by following their brilliant-white rear end.

Another potential sighting to be on the alert for is the pine marten. It is a cat-sized member of the weasel family. It is body is 65 to 70 cm long and is covered in dark brown fur with a white creamy patch at its throat. They have been spotted across east Dunbartonshire. Sightings have been reported of the pine marten on the Douglas Muir and the scats it leaves behind. I know, I know, but somebody has to examine its DNA.

Pine Marten
Photograph: Willie Anderson

Continue until you come to a kissing gate. The initial path on the other side of the gate can be a little muddy until you reach the boardwalk. Carry on uphill towards the pylon where the path broadens. As you reach the high ground you can now see the activity in the quarry. The path starts to decline and at the junction veer right towards the tunnel. This part can be wet and muddy. The tunnel has been constructed to allow the quarry vehicles to pass safely overhead. When you come out of the tunnel continue along the boardwalk and then on to a path made from

The Tunnel, Douglas Muir
Photograph: Iain MacVoy

Chapter 8. Hardgate to Stockiemuir Road

aggregate. A drainage ditch has been dug on the left side. Further on there is a fenced path leading to a viewing gallery.

This allows a clear view of the machines drilling and biting into the hillside and the large trucks ferrying away the produce. Sand and gravel were discovered in 1970 and the quarry opened in 1973. Sand and gravel are dug up and crushed in the quarry machinery. Building merchants, concrete makers and the public buy the products. Your driveway may have been quarried here.

The sand and gravel came during the Ice Age when a glacier transported them here and the meltwater deposited them when the ice melted, possibly 10,000 years ago.

A large number of trees has been planted in this area that should absorb water and encourage wildlife. After completion of the work, there will be restitution carried out with the possible construction of a nature reserve.

Throughout the walk across the Muir you can see the Kilpatrick Hills that stretch from Dumbarton in the west to Strathblane in the east. Strathblane divides the Kilpatricks from the Campsie Fells further to the east. The majority of the Kilpatrick Hills are within West Dunbartonshire, although they extend to the East Dunbartonshire and Stirlingshire areas. The highest points in the range are Duncolm (1,314 ft / 401 m) and Fynloch (1,313 ft / 400 m).

The Kilpatricks are part of the Clyde Plateau Lavas and are about 340 million years old. They take their name from the village of Old Kilpatrick that lies at their southern foot.

Carry on back on the path and pass over a small bridge with the sound of a babbling burn beneath your feet. Pass through another gate and on to a small section of walkway. Straight ahead there is a large dyke, sturdy steps provided. Once on the other side continue

Clyde Coastal Path Guidebook

straight ahead over a path that can be muddy then turn right along an ancient tree lined route slightly downhill.

You could just imagine travelling down this path on horseback with a fair maiden riding alongside, the scent of romance in the air. Perhaps, on second thoughts, given the cattle in the fields nearby, it is probably a different scent altogether invading the senses.

At the end of the path there is a gate ahead. There is also one on the right leading to a well-formed path to Tambowie Farm. Ignore the latter! Go straight ahead through the kissing gate to the left of the large metal gate and carry on downhill keeping close to the fence and Cauldstream Burn on the left. Pass through the kissing gate and continue down the path between the house on right and the burn on the left. This path can be wet and slippery, particularly over exposed stone. Just before the bottom as you pass between the houses there is a drop of less than 1 metre with four steps cut in the rock. To the right, just as you reach the Stockiemuir Road (A809) is the old Craigton Primary School House.

Steps at Cauldstream Burn
Photograph: Iain R White

TRAFFIC ALERT!
Take care on the Stockiemuir Road - speedy traffic.

Chapter 8. Hardgate to Stockiemuir Road

Pine Marten

Rotary are partners in community projects:
Milngavie Youth Centre
and the Waypoint.

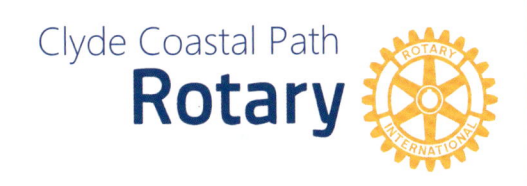

Clyde Coastal Path
Rotary

Clyde Coastal Path Guidebook

9. Craigton to Milngavie

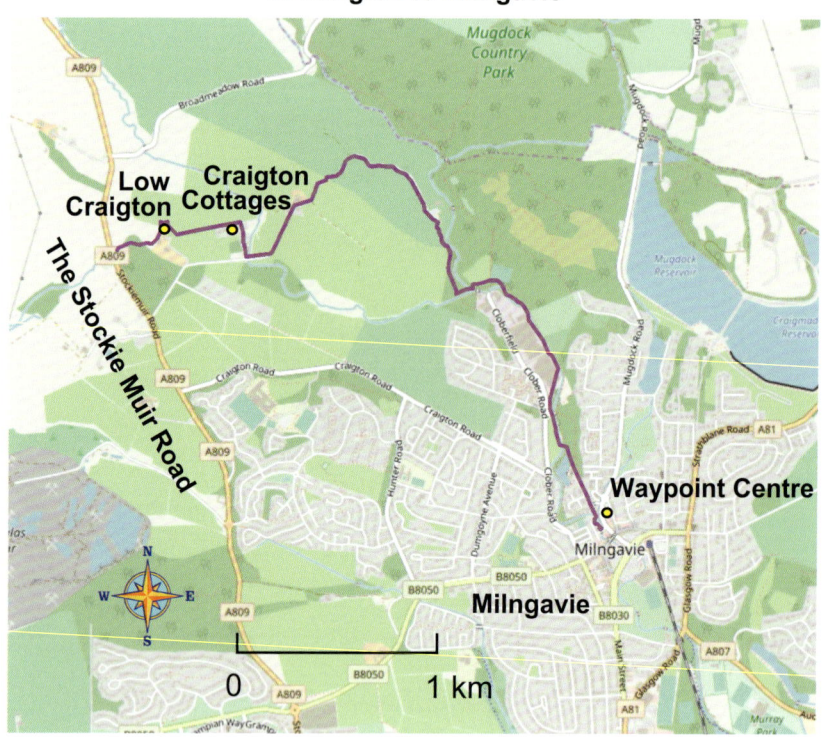

Chapter 9. Craigton to Milngavie

9. Craigton to Milngavie

Cross carefully over the Stockiemuir Road into the wooded area and follow the path that can be muddy. Bear right with the path then, at the signpost, bear left and exit the wood through the kissing gate. The path begins to climb steeply towards a fence. Follow the fence along the wall of Low Craigton Farm. At the corner turn right and follow the back wall. At the end of the wall, turn right and cross the dyke through the kissing gate about 30 m from the corner. Turn right alongside the far side of the dyke and follow the dyke to the end where you turn left and follow the path to the end of that wall. Now turn left and head out across the field towards Craigton Cottages.

Wood, East of Old School House
Photograph: Iain R White

The area to the right, before and after the cottages is the site of the Craigton Bleachfields and Bleach Works. The bleach fields were worked, for much of the mid and late 19th century and the first part of the 20th century, by the Blackwood family. Previously, they had been managed by David Dunlop and family until his death in 1842. The bleachfields were fields where cloth was spread out and bleached by the sun or by water, having been treated with alkali and acid agents. Over to the right, before the cottages is where the dam used by the works was situated but the retained loch is now filled in. The bleaching process took months and required large areas of land. Although by 1860, the Craigton Bleach Works were described as an establishment composed of stone buildings for bleaching cotton, they were still referred to as fields although the work had been speeded up by the invention of bleaching powder and the use of steam thereby reducing the need for bleach fields. The Works were powered by the Craigton Burn on its way down to join the Allander Water in Milngavie.

The workers in the Bleach Works came from Clydebank, Duntocher, Hardgate and Faifley on foot across the Bankie Trail to reach Craigton. Some carried on to Milngavie. The men did this twice per day. The women, however, were allowed to stay in the "wummin's hooses' from Monday to Friday. These are now Craigton Cottages.

In 1949, the Craigton Bleach Works, by then the Craigton Bleaching Company, went into liquidation.

Pass through the gate and walk on the grass that runs along the back of the gardens of the cottages. Many do not have a fence between the garden and the path and have also developed the ground to the left of the path. This gives the impression of walking through their back gardens.

At the end of the grassy path turn right and continue, to meet the access road to the cottages. Pass the offices on the left and near the bottom Craigton Industries Ltd. Turn left on to The Loan, a winding single-track private road leading through Laighpark Farm and shortly after, Milngavie Golf Course.

Milngavie Golf Course was founded in 1895 initially as a nine hole course although it quickly became an eighteen hole course. The course was leased until purchased in 1927 by the members. The original clubhouse built in 1895 was replaced in 1939.

Having survived errant golf balls, continue past the clubhouse on the left and the flagpole on the right and into the golf club car park. The route leaves the car park by the far left corner. Follow the path and for the first time you meet The Allander Water. After about 100 m, stop.

Chapter 9. Craigton to Milngavie

The Allander Water

Photograph: Peter Smith

The Allander Water is formed from small rivers around Auld Murroch Farm and runs through Milngavie and continues until it joins the River Kelvin as one of its three main tributaries; the other two are the Glazert Water and the Luggie Water. Where does the River Kelvin end up? Yes, you guessed it, the River Clyde at the Yorkhill Basin.

There is a manufactured weir, enlarged to form a Victorian swimming pool. Get your costumes out. Fifty metres further on is a cascade of water called, Jenny's Linn. A linn is a waterfall or pool at the bottom of it. Why Jenny? Who knows? One of Greenock's favourite sons, James Watt, and his father-in-law, Lord James McGrigor, owner of the Clober Bleach Field, built a weir at this site. A shutter was built to divert the water under the path beneath your feet. To the right you can see the exit site or, using the Scots word, cundy. This led the water to the "long race" along which the water ran to the man made dam that fed the Clober Bleach Works. James

Clyde Coastal Path Guidebook

Watt became aware of the work of Berthollet on chlorine as a bleaching agent, and enabled his father-in-law to utilise chlorine for the first time in the UK. Chlorine allowed activities to be undertaken quickly and cheaply, resulting in increased productivity and income.

In tribute to James Watt and Lord McGrigor, each has a street named after them in Milngavie .

You have a choice here. You can follow the path straight ahead leading through a wooded area alongside the Allander. Towards the end of the path it diverts from the Allander water and across a bridge over the Craigton Burn. Over the bridge turn left and follow the path to the Staney Brig. This is the site of the confluence of the Craigton Burn and the Allander Water. From here it continues as the Allander Water.

On the other hand, consider the alternative route and follow the "long race". About 10 to 15 ft after passing through the wall turn to the right and follow the narrow path. Continue along the path as it curves through the bushes and trees and enjoy the assault on your senses by the wildlife until you reach the bridge over the Craigton Burn as it makes its way down to meet the Allander Water.

Craigton Burn Meets the Allander Water
Photograph: Iain R White

Here there is evidence of a sluice directing water from the Craigton Burn down to feed the Clober Dam. The Craigton Burn has already provided power to the Craigton Bleach Works and has also supplied the water required at the Tambowie Distillery. Thousands of litres of water are required in the mashing , diluting and cooling processes.

Chapter 9. Craigton to Milngavie

Bridge over the Craigton Burn   Photograph: Peter Smith

There are suggestions that distilling was taking place in Tambowie in the early 18th century. Official distilling began with the Tambowie distillery in 1924. Alexander Graham owned the distillery from 1827 until his death in 1861, when it passed to his grandson Alexander Graham Buchanan. After his bankruptcy in 1885, it passed over the years to several different companies. In 1905, mid morning, there was an explosion and fire at the brick-built bonded warehouse and store, caused by a tipped paraffin lamp. The whole stock in the warehouse, 2000 casks of whisky, was destroyed, apart from 20 casks. Fortunately there were no fatalities or injuries. A second warehouse remained unscathed.

Not only did the warehouse catch fire but also a myth. A local man wrote a poem that was published in the Milngavie Herald about how he would picture the scene if the whisky had been tipped into the burn during the fire. Fertile imaginations over decades joined in the

Clyde Coastal Path Guidebook

spirit of this mouth-watering tale and elevated it to a fact.

In 1910, production ceased at the Tambowie Distillery. During its demolition in 1920, a wall collapsed on to two men and a boy, burying them. One man died at the scene and one was seriously injured. The boy escaped unharmed.

Look out for the dipper in the Craigton Burn. This stout little bird with long legs can be seen bobbing up and down on rocks in the water to feed on insects. It often cocks its tail. There will be further opportunities to see our white-bibbed friend along the Allander, where it can be seen walking underwater, even when it is fast flowing. It is the only bird that does this. It stops itself from floating to the surface by digging its toes into the bed of the river. The dipper's short wings are adapted for swimming, and it oils and waterproofs its feathers by means of a large preening gland. It can remain underwater for about 30 seconds. This is due to the fact that it as a higher haemoglobin than other birds and therefore has a greater oxygen carrying capacity. The dipper also has enhanced underwater vision, due to the well developed muscles in its eyes that can change the curvature of the lens.

Heron
Photograph: Vincent Cuddihy

Cross the bridge and take the path straight ahead. Stay on this path through the bushes until you reach a large grassy area with some trees.

Chapter 9. Craigton to Milngavie

The Precinct, Milngavie
Photograph: Iain R White

This is the site of the Clober Dam. People used to visit the Dam and have picnics and walks around it. In the 1950s, it was filled in and is now a park area.

Cross to the path and turn left. Continue to the first junction and turn right. Follow this path, passing the Allander Bus Company Depot. You now join the main route again at the Staney Brig. From here there is a clear view of the confluence of the Craigton Burn and the Allander Water. Cross over the bridge and turn right to join the path through Allander Park alongside the Allander Water.

There is a number of woodland birds to see and mallard ducks on the water. Look out for some gems. If alert, you may catch the blue flash of the elusive kingfisher. Then there is the heron, patiently standing at the edge of the river on its long legs and with a long elegant neck. At other times it's on a rock, its neck disappearing under hunched shoulders. During its slow flapping flight with its neck forming an S-bend, it loses some of its poise. As they say in ballroom dancing circles, "You'll need to work on your topline, Heron". Woodland birds are also in abundance. In spring, there is an opportunity to see the fiery-breasted bullfinch. They are shy birds and tend to travel in pairs, however, they can be seen in family parties after the breeding season. They love the buds of fruit trees.

Carry on following the path with the Allander on your right. Across the water and through the trees you can see the businesses and light

Clyde Coastal Path Guidebook

industry still thriving by the Allander. Eventually you reach the Iron Bridge with the access cobbles forming a thistle pattern. Cross over to look at another important site.

At the other side there is evidence of the sluice that diverted water through the Cloberfield to the site of The Allander Bleaching Company and West of Scotland Laundry, about a quarter of a mile away. It ceased trading soon after the end of World War Two. The poppy monuments in the Cloberfield are commemorating the dead of World Wars One and Two.

Step into the car park to your right. Across the road you can see one of the pillars that marked the entrance to the Clober Estate and Clober House. The house was demolished to make way for new housing. To the right of the pillar, the houses are built on the site of the Clober Bleach Works discussed earlier.

Cross back over the bridge and turn right and follow the path to Milngavie.

On your left for the next half mile you will see slopes, many of them steep, that are covered in trees, bushes and flowers. These slopes are lime dumps. Lime was heavily used in the making of paper at the Ellangowan Paper Mill whose site you will see shortly. Thousands upon thousands of lime residue were deposited over this area, resulting in a rich, fertile ground able to support a large number of trees, shrubs and flowers. These include a variety of orchids. There is a plentiful supply of the Common Twayblade Orchid (Neottia ovata), easily recognised by the very distinctive double leaf at its base, and until recently, the Common Spotted Orchid (Dactylorhiza fuchsii), and Broad-

Common Twayblade Orchid
Photograph: Vincent Cuddihy

Chapter 9. Craigton to Milngavie

leaved Hellebore (epipactis helleborine). There may still be some of the latter two in the dense growth over this large area.

There is evidence of community life in the area of Milngavie as far back as the Bronze Age. Several finds from that time, including a cist, were discovered on the north end of the Barloch Housing Estate. Before the Romans came, (remember them?), the area around Milngavie was ruled by a powerful tribe called the Danni. One of the forts on Antonine's Wall was situated at neighbouring Bearsden. When the Romans left, a period of instability followed as Pictish tribes from the north repeatedly invaded, leading to battles for supremacy.

The population of Milngavie in 1793 was only 200. During the Industrial Revolution its numbers increased and in 1870 had risen to over 2000. In the census of 2001, it was recorded as having a population of 12,759 in 5,256 households. In its industrial heyday it possessed a cotton mill that became a paper mill, a bleachworks, dyeworks and a grain mill.

Why is Milngavie so called? Many heads more learned than mine have been thoroughly scratched for decades over this question. Its first industry was a grain mill. This building, Gavin's Mill, still stands and is one of Milngavie's oldest buildings. One school of thought is that this is the origin of the village's name. That same school of thought, however, fails to explain who Gavin was. Local people, however, used to refer to this mill as Watt's Mill, after James Watt and his family who were heavily associated with the mill. It is important to note that this is NOT the same James Watt renowned for his engineering feats. Gavin's Mill still stands along with its wheel and was renovated in the 1960s by a local architect Bert Morris. The ground floor was Gavin's Mill Tearoom and the upper floor was his office. It has undergone several changes of ownership and use since then and is now a fairtrade shop and tearoom. A charitable organisation, The Gavin's Mill Project, has been set up to oversee the running of the enterprise.

Clyde Coastal Path Guidebook

The Waypoint, Milngavie
Sponsored by Allander Rotary
Photograph:Granville Fox

Let us now turn to the Gaelic derivation. Get out your notebook and pen and take a deep breath; here goes. The Scots Gaelic for a mill is muileann and is pronounced "moolun". The Gaelic for David is "Daibhidh", for which there are two different pronunciations, one of which is "daa-ee". A noun in the genitive preceded by another noun is aspirated, hence "Daibhidh" is changed to "Dhaibhidh". "Dh" and "gh" sound alike in Gaelic, hence Muileann Dhaibhidh came to be pronounced as "mulnngai", the two syllables of muileann being run together because the stress is on the second word, and thus we have "Mulguy". This suggests that "Gavin's Mill" is incorrect as the origin of the name and that it derives from the Gaelic for "David's Mill". We do know that there was a mill in Strathblane known as Milndavie.

There will be an exam on this subject at the end of the walk.

Continue until you reach the pond at the Library and Community Centre. This is an old mill pond.

This was the site of Milngavie Cotton Spinning Mill built in 1775. Between 1861 and 1865, during the American Civil War, the cotton industry in the UK suffered a "cotton famine" as the imports of raw cotton were severely affected. In 1866, it was bought by William

Chapter 9. Craigton to Milngavie

Whyte and converted into The Allander Paper Mill. By 1882, the paper mill was ailing and Colonel John Birrell stepped in and bought the struggling mill and renamed it, The Ellangowan Paper Mill. He died age 63 in 1920 when the running of the mill was taken over by his step-brother and a board of directors. In 1949 it was absorbed by the Clyde Paper Company. It finally closed in 1971.

Follow the path to the left through a wooded area and at the junction turn right and continue along the path.

This final stretch of path is built on an old railway line. The paper mill had its own sidings running up from Milngavie Station to the mill, allowing it to unload the raw materials and load the paper for distribution. The single track railway line ran on for another half mile to carry the lime to the dumps. The Waypoint is an information centre just on the opposite side of Ellangowan Road. There are public toilets in nearby Milngavie Youth Centre.

A little further on and then it's "Welcome to Milngavie".

"Shall I find comfort, travel sore and weak?
Of labour you shall find the sum.
Will there be beds for me and all who seek?
Yea, beds for all who come."
"Uphill"

Christina Rosetti

There are many places to recharge with food and drink and plan your next walk. Since you are now at the gateway to the West Highland Way, problem solved. Perhaps you may be wise to rest at one of the local hotels or boarding houses before you make that journey.

Clyde Coastal Path Guidebook

Greenock Cut with House for Waster

Photograph: Jim Blair

The Lyle Kirk, Greenock Esplanade

Photograph: John MacLeod

Erskine Bridge from the PS Waverley

Photograph: David Palmar photoscot.co.uk

Appendix I. Further Connections

Appendix I. Further Connections

International Appalachian Trail - Scotland
www.iat-sia.com

A. Firth o Clyde Rotary Trail (Opened 9 May 2015)

www.focrt.org

FoCRT as created by four Rotary Clubs between 2008 and 2014, linking with IAT Ireland across the North Channel. It forms the first section of the International Appalachian Trail Scotland and runs from the Mull of Galloway to Cape Wrath.

FoCRT runs from the Mull of Galloway to Milngavie, a distance of 171 miles miles (279 km), and is a partnership of three autonomous long-distance routes, LDRs).

1. Mull of Galloway Trail: (Opened August 2012)

mgt.focrt.org

The Mull of Galloway Trail, constructed by the Rotary Club of Stranraer, stretches for 24 miles from the Mull lighthouse to Stranraer. There it links up with the 12 mile long Loch Ryan Coastal Path to Glenapp. The Stranraer Rotary also constructed this path. At Glenapp, it links with the Ayrshire Coastal Path. Total distance 36 miles (60 km)

The Trail offers fine views of The Galloway Hills and the Machars coastline. From the Mull of Galloway, the English Lake District Fells, the Isle of Man, the Mountains of Mourne and the Irish Coast can be seen.

Clyde Coastal Path Guidebook

Near Stranraer, it crosses the Southern Upland Way and follows the Coastal Path along Loch Ryan and climbs up to high muirlands with views of loch, sea and hills.

The diversity of the landscape provides habitat for a variety of wildlife, including birds and flora.

2. Ayrshire Coastal Path: (Opened June 2008)

acp.focrt.org

The Ayrshire Coastal Path, marked out and signposted by the Rotary Club of Ayr, runs for 100 miles (161 km) from Glenapp to Skelmorlie. It has a diverse terrain, travelling over miles of tracks, proms, beaches and field-edge paths. The Path offers beautiful views along the coast of the Clyde. Ailsa Craig and the Kintyre peninsula in the Lower Firth of Clyde succeeded by the hills of Arran and then the Isles of Cumbrae and Bute as we reach the Upper Firth of Clyde. There is a huge range of historical sites and a wide variety of bird life.

3. Clyde Coastal Path: (Opened June 2014)

ccp.focrt.org

Distance by high muirland route 37 miles (60 km)

Distance by low coastal route 41 miles (65 km)

Appendix I. Further Connections

B. West Highland Way

www.west-highland-way.co.uk

This begins at Milngavie, and runs for 96 miles (154 km) along Loch Lomond and over Rannoch Muir by Glencoe to Fort William.

C. Cape Wrath Trail

www.capewrathtrail.org.uk

www.capewrathtrailguide.org/route

This is a 220 mile (350 km) unmarked trail, from Fort William to Cape Wrath, for the well equipped, experienced walker. There is no officially sanctioned route for the trail.

D. John Galt Way

The John Galt Way, linking Irvine and Greenock, the towns where the author was born and died, partly follows the Clyde Coastal Path, but takes an alternative route between Inverkip and Greenock – one followed by the characters of his first major novel, "The Ayrshire Legatees" (1820).

Clyde Coastal Path Guidebook

The Partick Spur Ends at Boden Boo   Photograph: Iain R White

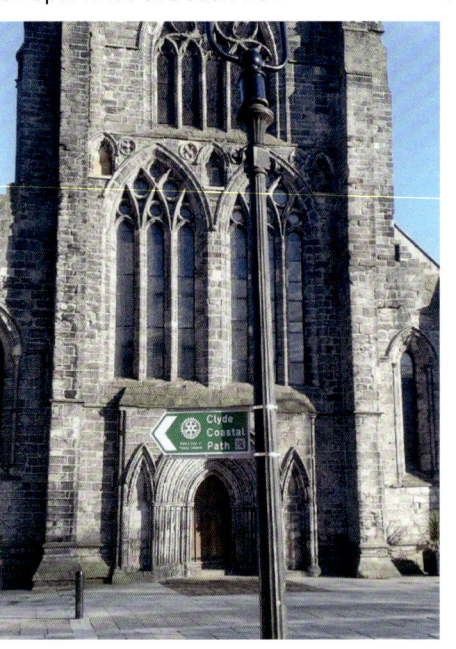

The Paisley Spur Starts at Paisley Abbey
Photograph: Gordon Russell

Appendix II. Further Developments

A. Path Development

The Rotary Club of Govan, the Rotary Club of Renfrew and the Rotary Club of Erskine have added the Partick Spur from Partick railway station, Glasgow, at the end of the Clyde Walkway, to Boden Boo.

The spur is in three parts:
- Partick Station to King George V Dock
- King George V Dock to the two Rivers Cart
- Rivers Cart to Boden Boo.

The Rotary Club of Paisley Callants has added the Paisley Spur from Paisley Abbey to the Rivers Cart.

B. IT Development

At present all the signs have a QR code. Eventually the posts to which they are attached will also have a Mini QR code and Near Field Communication (NFC).

Any one of these can be used by the walker to discover the walker's position and progress by time and distance along the path.

Clyde Coastal Path Guidebook

Appendix III. Rotary Family and CCP Board

The Rotary Family

ROTAKIDS Ages 7 - 11 years. Partnership with local schools

INTERACT Ages 12 – 18 years. Projects with Secondary schools

ROTARACT Ages 18 - 24 years. Stand alone with Rotary support

ROTARY Aged 24+. The lead club in an area supporting all the clubs.

Clyde Coastal Path Board

The Board consists of representatives of the following Clubs

Allander Rotary (Bearsden and Milngavie) was founded in May 1970 and meets every Thursday evening at the Glasgow Golf Club.

Gourock Rotary was established 42 years ago in May 1976 and meets in Royal Gourock Yacht Club every Thursday evening.

Erskine and District Rotary founded in 2002 meets every Monday evening in the Ingliston Equestrian Centre, Bishopton.

Govan Rotary has been in existence since 1953 and meets in the Morton Suite Restaurant in Ibrox Football Stadium every Monday lunchtime.

Paisley Callants Rotary was formed in 1982 and meets every Monday evening in the Glynhill Hotel, Renfrew.

Renfrew Rotary, founded in 1952, meets at Ralston Golf Club, Paisley, every Tuesday evening.

To find out more about Rotary and Clubs near you, visit
www.rotarygbi.org.

Clyde Coastal Path

Index

1
1711 28
1797 23
1820 .... 61, 121
1829 23
1889 28
1894 26
1895 23
1897 23
1900 27
1902 27
1907 30
1908 27
1909 27
1910 30
1931 23
1956 25
1959 30
1977 25
1990s 23

3
3000 BCE 75

A
A770 23
A8 77
A809 104
A815 77
Abhainn Chluaidh 11
acetylene 23
Achadh na Creag 99
Acts of Union 18
Adams and McLean 35
Admiralty 30
Ailsa Craig 120
Akka, MV 25

Clyde Coastal Path Guidebook

Albert Harbour.. 33
Allander Bleaching Company.. 114
Allander Bus Company.. 113
Allander Park.. 113
Allander Water.. 113
American Civil War.. 100
Amundsen, Roald.. 33
Annals of the Parish.. 75
Antarctica.. 33
Appalachian Trail, International.. 119
Ardgowan Estate... 19
Ardgowan Fishery.. 47
Argyll.. 21, 27, 36, 50, 65, 68, 74
Arran.. 17
Arrol, Sir William.. 55
Arthur's Brae... 99
auk... 25
Auld Murroch Farm.. 109
Ayrshire.. 4
Ayrshire Coastal Path.. 9, 119-120
Ayrshire Legatees, The.. 121

B

basking shark... 20
Battery Park... 30
Beeches Road... 95
Berthollet... 110
Big Wood... 77
Birrell, Colonel John... 117
Bishopton.. 75
Blackmore.. 35
Blantyre, Lord.. 91
Boden Boo.. 123
Bower Hills.. 33
Bowers, Henry "Birdie".. 33
Britannia.. 89
Bronze Age.. 97
Broomielaw Quay... 28
bullfinch... 113

Clyde Coastal Path

Burns, Robert... 44
Bute, Isle of... 21
buzzard... 21

C

Caisteal Abhail.. 17
Caledonian MacBrayne....................................... 28, 30
Caledonian Railway... 28
Caledonian Steam Packet Company....................... 28
Calmac.. 30
Campbell, Mary.. 44
Cape Wrath Trail... 121
Cappielow Park.. 58
Captayannis... 51
Cardwell Garden Centre... 21
Carleith Road... 88
Cart, River.. 123
Cartsburn... 35
Cartsdyke... 35
Castle Gardens.. 28
Catacol... 17
Caulder's Garden Centre... 81
Cauldstream Burn.. 104
Chartroom Restaurant.. 19
Chicago.. 12
chiffchaff.. 44
Cloberfield.. 114
Cloch Lighthouse... 23
Cloch lighthouse.. 24
Cloch Point.. 23, 25
Cloch Road.. 23, 26
Clyde.. 11
Clyde Coastal Path.. 4
Clyde Paper Company... 117
Clyde Walkway... 123
Clydebank.. 55
Coats, James... 27
Cochno... 97
Cochno Burn.. 95

Clyde Coastal Path Guidebook

Cochno Loch.. 97
Cochno Road... 101
Cochno Stone.. 97
Comet... 62
Corbett.. 17
Cormorants... 25
Cornalees.. 46
Cowal.. 21
Cowan's Corner... 52
Cowshed.. 58
Craigs Avenue.. 95
Craigton Bleach Works... 110
Craigton Burn... 110
Craigton Cottages... 107
Crawhin Hill.. 46
Crawhin Reservoir.. 46
Crinan Canal.. 61
Cumbrae, Isle of... 16
curlew... 20

D

Daer Water... 11
Dalmuir... 91
Dalnottar... 96
Dalziel, Alexander... 71
dipper... 112
doon the watter.. 28
Douglas Muir.. 99
Douglas Muir Road... 99
Drummond Funeral Directors... 95
Drumry... 96
Duchess of Hamilton.. 28
duck... 113
Dumbarton... 73
Dumbarton Castle.. 73
Dumbarton Rock.. 73
Duncolm... 103
Dunglas.. 63
Dunlop, David.. 107

Dunn, William... 96
dunnock... 43
Dunoon... 24, 25, 30
Dunrod... 18
Dunrod Castle... 18
Duntocher... 97

E
Edward VII, King.. 27
Ellangowan Paper Mill... 117
Erskine Bridge.. 78
Erskine Golf Course... 78
Erskine Home Farm... 77
Erskine House.. 77
Esplanade... 22, 23, 27, 31

F
Faifley... 97
Faifley Knowes.. 99
Faifley Road... 99
Fergusons.. 57
Ferry Road... 77
Finlaystone Estate... 71
Finnieston.. 55
Firth of Forth.. 16
FoCRT, Firth o Clyde Rotary Trail...................................... 119
Fort Matilda... 30
Fort William... 121
Fynloch.. 103

G
Gaelic... 11, 16, 23, 28, 38, 73, 90, 95, 99
Gallagher, Eric... 21
Galloway.. 119
Galt Fountain... 33
Galt, John.. 75
Gantocks... 24
Gantocks light... 24
Gantocks reef.. 24

Gaoda Bheinn	17
Gareloch	51
Gartclash	96
Gavin's Mill	115
geese	47
George V Dock, King	123
Glazert Water	109
Glen Sannox	28
Glenapp	119-120
Glencairn	71
Glencoe	121
Goatfell	17
goldeneye	68
Goldenhill Park	95
goosander	47
Gourock	50
Gourock Railway Station	27
Gourock Rope Works	28
Gourock Sailing Club	26
Gourock Yacht Club	27
Graham, Alexander	111
Granny Kempock's Stone	28
Greenock	50
Greenock Cut	46
Greenock Cut Centre	45
guillemot	20

H

Hardgate	95
Hardgate Knowes	95
Hardgate Mill	96
Harris, Paul	12
Harvey, Rev James, of Duntocher	97
Hatton Brae	75
Helensburgh	60
Henry Bell	60, 63
heron	113
Highland Boundary Fault	44
Highland Mary	44

Hippocrates 12
Hunter's Quay 25

I

Ice Age 103
Innellan 21
Inverkip 18
Ionnis, Captain Theodorakis 51
Iron Bridge 114

J

James IV, King 28
Jenny's Linn 109
John Galt Way 121

K

Kelburn Park 67
Kelly Burn 4
Kelly Cut 43
Kelly Glen 43
Kelly Reservoir 46
Kempock Point 62
Kempock Street 28
kestrel 47
Kilcreggan 27, 29
Kilcreggan Ferry 27, 30
Kilpatrick Hills 95
Kincaids 35
kingfisher 113
Kintyre 120
Kip Marina 19
Klondyke 35
Knappes Farm 96
Knox, John 71

L

Laighpark Farm 108
Lake District Fells 119
Lamont 35

Clyde Coastal Path Guidebook

Langbank... 72
lapwing.. 20
Largs... 16
Linlithgow.. 60
Lithgow Way... 63
Little Cumbrae.. 25
Loch Craignish... 61
Loch Lomond... 121
Loch Long... 25
Loch Ryan.. 120
Loch Ryan Coastal Path.. 119
Loch Thom... 35
Lochranza... 17
Low Coastal Route... 15
Low Craigton Farm.. 107
Luggie Water.. 109
Lunderston Bay... 20, 22, 23

M

M8.. 77
MacMillan, Gordon... 71
Magnusson,Sally.. 9
Man, Isle of 119
Mar Hall.. 78
martin, house 47
Mary, Queen of Scots.. 74
Maxwell, Sir Patrick.. 66
McCaskie, Mearns T.. 48
McColl, Jim.. 65
McGrigor, Lord James.. 109
McInroy's Point.. 25
Meall Mòr... 17
Miller, James.. 16
Millport... 16
Milngavie... 4, 101, 106-111, 114-117, 119
Motherwell.. 55
Mountblow.. 96
Mourne, Mountains of 119
Muirshiel Regional Park... 18

Clyde Coastal Path

Mull of Galloway Trail 9, 119

N
Napoleon's navy 30
North Porteous Road 77

O
Ocean Terminal 51
Olaf the White 75
Old Greenock Road 77
orca 26
oystercatcher 20

P
Paisley Abbey 123
Paisley Spur 4, 123
Parklea 68
Partick 123
Partick Spur 4, 123
Paterson, Gil, MSP 98
peewit 21
peregrine 47
pigeon 43
Pine Marten 102
pine marten 102
pipit 46
porpoise 20
Port Glasgow 28
Potrail Water 11

Q
Queen Mary II, TS 28

R
Rankine 35
Rannoch Muir 121
razorbill 20
redshank 20
Renfrew 56

Clyde Coastal Path Guidebook

River Clyde.. 11
robin... 43
Rochead, John Thomas.. 96
Rotary Club of Allander.. 12
Rotary Club of Ayr.. 120
Rotary Club of Erskine... 123
Rotary Club of Gourock.. 27
Rotary Club of Govan... 123
Rotary Club of Paisley Callants.. 123
Rotary Club of Renfrew.. 123
Rotary Club of Stranraer.. 119
Rothesay... 15
Royal Arsenal, Woolwich.. 30
Royal Yacht Club.. 26
Running the lights... 25

S

Scots.. 11, 21, 72, 99, 109
Scott, Captain... 33
Scotts... 33, 35, 41, 55
Shaw Stewarts.. 35
shearwater.. 25
Shielhill Farm.. 18
Skelmorlie... 44
Sleeping Warrior... 17
Smirkie, Sir Robert.. 78
Smith, Robert.. 23
South Pole.. 33
St John's Church.. 28
St Mirren... 58
Staney Brig... 113
Stevenson, Robert.. 23
Stevenson, Robert Louis.. 23
Stockiemuir Road... 104
stonechat.. 46
Stranraer... 120
Strathclyde.. 75
Stuart, Robert Walter, 11th Lord Blantyre.................................. 77
sugar ship... 51

Sutherland Upland Way.. 120
swallow... 47
Swallow Road... 99
swan.. 68
swift... 47
Symington, William.. 60

T

Tail o the Bank... 51
Tambowie.. 110
Tartaglia, Philip.. 72
Tate and Lyle Westburn Refinery....................................... 51
tern.. 25
Terra Nova.. 33
Thom, Robert... 48
thrush.. 43
Tighnabruaich.. 16
tit... 43
Titan Crane.. 102
Torpedo Experimental Establishment................................ 30
Torpedo Factory.. 30
torpedo factory.. 30
Torphichen Mill.. 60
Toward Point... 44

V

Valve House... 49
Victoria Harbour.. 33
Victoria Tower... 52
vicus... 87

W

Wallace, Robert of Kelly... 15
waster... 49
Watermeetings.. 11
Watt, James... 50
Waverley, PS... 25
Waypoint and Information Centre........................... 105, 116
Wellpark Mid Kirk... 52

Clyde Coastal Path Guidebook

Wemyss Bay... 43
West Highland Way.. 121
West of Scotland Amateur Sailing Club...................................... 31
Westburn Church... 52
whinchat.. 46
Whitehill... 101
Whiteinch.. 55
Whitemoss Farm... 75
Whyte, William.. 116
William Street.. 34
Woodhall Roundabout... 71
World War One... 11, 55, 57, 92
World War Two............... 11, 24, 30, 52, 76, 91, 95, 100, 101, 114
wren.. 43

Y

Yorkhill Basin.. 109

Common Dolphin   Photograph: David Palmar
                                                                    photoscot.co.uk

Clyde Coastal Path

List of Images

Forward!	2
Selection of Signs	13
Wemyss Bay Station	15
New Arrivals	16
Kip Marina	19
Lunderston Bay	20
Peewit	20
Buzzard Hovering	21
The Cloch Light	24
PS Waverley	26
Granny Kempock's Stone	29
Manx Shearwater	31
John Galt Fountain	34
Arms of Greenock	35
View from the Lyle Hill	37
Greenock	39
The Custom House, Greenock	40
Long-tailed Tit	43
Great Spotted Woodpecker	44
The Kelly Cut	45
Goosander	47
The Greenock Cut Centre	48
The Greenock Cut	49
Rhu & Gare Loch from Overton Road	50
The PS Waverley under the Erskine Bridge	53
Titan Crane at James Watt Dock	55
Bollards at James Watt Dock	57
James Watt	61
The Comet	62
Newark Castle	66
Timber Ponds at Park Lea	67
Oyster Catcher Flock in Flight	69
Approaching Langbank	72
Path, East of Langbank	73
Dumbarton Rock	74
Erskine Bridge on a Wet Day	79
The Path through Boden Boo	81
The Erskine Bridge	83

Clyde Coastal Path Guidebook

List of Images (continued)

The Kilpatrick Hills from the Path	85
Tree at Dalnottar Cemetery	86
The Opening of the Thomas Wood Path	88
A Quiet Path Just North of the Busy A82	93
Path, Just West of Dalnottar Cemetery	93
Cup & Ring Markings, Cochno	97
Cup and Ring Marks	98
Whitehill Farm Path	101
Pine Marten	102
The Tunnel, Douglas Muir	102
Steps at Cauldstream Burn	104
Pine Marten	105
Wood, East of Old School House	107
The Allander Water	109
Craigton Burn Meets the Allander Water	110
Bridge over the Craigton Burn	111
Heron	112
The Precinct, Milngavie	113
Common Twayblade Orchid	114
The Waypoint, Milngavie Sponsored by Allander Rotary	116
We're done!	117
Erskine Bridge from the PS Waverley	118
The Lyle Kirk, Greenock Esplanade	118
Greenock Cut with House for Waster	118
The Paisley Spur Starts at Paisley Abbey	122
The Partick Spur Ends at Boden Boo	122
Common Dolphin	136

List of Maps

1. Wemyss Bay to Lunderston Bay - Coastal Route	14
2. Lunderston Bay to Greenock Esplanade	22
3. Greenock Esplanade to Victoria Harbour	32
4. Wemyss Bay to Victoria Harbour Muirland Route	42
5. Victoria Harbour to Woodhall Roundabout	54
6. Woodhall Roundabout to Erskine Bridge	70
7. Erskine Bridge to Hardgate	82
8. Hardgate to the Stockiemuir Road	94
9. Craigton to Milngavie	106

Clyde Coastal Path

About the Author

Dr Vincent Cuddihy was President of the Rotary Club of Allander in 2011 - 2012 and in 2018 - 2019.

In a former life, he was a kenspeckled GP in Milngavie, where he still lives.

Now, he has become an Author.

From all these interests, he encourages you to get out there and walk the Clyde Coastal Path.

Glengoyne Distillery are pleased to have supported the Photographic Competition which contributed so many beautiful images to illustrate this Guidebook.

GLENGOYNE
HIGHLAND SINGLE MALT
SCOTCH WHISKY

Rotary initiated, and is a major contributor to, Shelter Boxes that are delivered around the world helping disaster areas.

Clyde Coastal Path
Rotary

Clyde Coastal Path Guidebook

Clyde Coastal Path Board

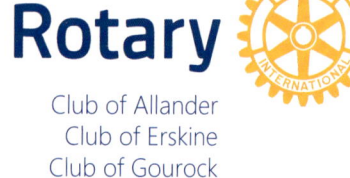

Rotary

Club of Allander
Club of Erskine
Club of Gourock
Club of Govan
Club of Paisley Callants
Club of Renfrew